In the Spirit of Love

Carver Alan Ames

In the Spirit of Love

Talks and interviews compiled
by Beatrix Zureich

© 2009 Carver Alan Ames
Sections of this book may not be copied without permission of the author.
www.alanames.org

Layout and design: Andreas Zureich, Switzerland
Printed in the United States of America

ISBN 978-0-9820329-3-0

After the success in touching lives of the book "Brought to life" which was a compilation of several of my talks and interviews it was decided to do another book along similar lines. Within this book are a mixture of recent talks and interviews on the wonderful grace God has been pouring into and out through my life.

As I read and reflect on the words I am deeply moved by the love, the tenderness and the kindness in which God reaches out to all of us. His words explain, sometimes in mystical and deeply spiritual ways but always with simplicity, the wonder of His love for mankind and how the fullness of His love can only be found in His Holy Catholic and Apostolic Church.

To me it is amazing that the almighty God would love mankind so much that He sent His only Son, Jesus, to suffer and die for us. This book helps bring a better understanding of the immeasurable love that God has for each one of us and in places, brings those who will be open to it, to a close relationship with Jesus on the cross of love.

As these are compilations of my talks some subjects are covered briefly due to time restraints. However, in my other books, especially "What is truth", some of these subjects can be read in more detail. Also it is encouraged that each one would read the Catechism of The Holy Catholic Church so as to understand Church teaching in these matters.

My hope is that all who read this book will benefit from the God-given words it contains. Realizing, apart from the descriptions of my life, they truly are not my words but those given through me by the Holy Spirit and will thank God, not me, for such a blessing of His love.

God love you,

Alan Ames

This transcript of a radio interview gives a short introduction on the background and the ministry.

Could you introduce yourself?

I come from Australia and I come spreading the love of God by the grace of God and with the support of Archbishop Barry Hickey of the Holy Catholic Church. I travel the world praying for healing and encouraging people to live the Catholic faith because heaven has shown me that this faith is the faith and the Church that Jesus Christ, Our Lord and Saviour, gave to mankind. So if I want to live fully His way, I have to be Catholic. Now my role in life is to go around and encourage people to be Catholic and to live the faith.

Did you find God or did God find you?

I certainly didn't find God, He found me because I had no thoughts of God. Through my blindness, through my hardened heart and my sin-filled soul, the Lord, Jesus, reached gently inside and by His grace drew me to Him. So it was nothing I did, it was all God did and I can never stop thanking Him for that.

What was your experience with God's love?

I have had many special experiences with God's love and I suppose the one people are most interested in is how God came into my life. It did not happen because I was someone special or because God loved me more than everyone else. It was because God loved me the same as everyone else He came into my life offering me salvation.

I think I was one of the worst sinners in the world committing just about every sin. I hurt so many people, emotionally and physically. I almost killed two or three and was addicted to many things. I led a life focused on myself and on the world. I truly did not believe in God. Like many of those who sin the way I did, I thought that God couldn't love me if He existed because I couldn't even love myself. At the age of forty, God decided to show me that He did exist and that He loved me and that He loved all people, even the worst sinner in the world. The only difference is how much we love God. God loves us all with a passionate love and His love is there for all. All that God desires is that people love Him.

I was told that He loved me just as I am with all my faults and weaknesses. Of course, He does not love the bad things I had done but always He loves the person. His love is constant, it is always there for every person. He denies no one His love but many people deny themselves God's love.

How was life before you got to know the love of God?

Before I knew God's love, my life was empty and meaningless. I lived a life full of sin and full of self and I lived the way of the world, never thinking about God, just thinking about pleasing myself. When I did get slight thoughts about Him, I just pushed them aside and focused just living for myself. No matter how I tried to find excitement and please myself, always there was an emptiness within that nothing in this world could fill. It was only when God's love came into my life, this emptiness was filled.

How did God first speak to you?

First He sent me an angel, then some saints, Our Lady and finally the Lord Himself came speaking and appearing to me.

God spoke to me about the longings people have inside of them. Explaining the longing God has is that every person would come and love Him. That every person through His Son and Our Lord, Jesus, would just come and truthfully say, "I am sorry, forgive me for what I have done." Then, in Him, they will find forgiveness and they will find God waiting to embrace them in love, not condemn them because that is all God offers us, love in Himself Who is love.

The Lord encouraged me to stop doing all the bad things and to start living in His love. By His grace, I managed to embrace Him and to my great surprise, I found that embracing Jesus brought me the deepest joy, the deepest happiness, the deepest love. It is a love, a joy, a happiness that is beyond anything of this world. Now, by living for Jesus each day, I experience these things every day and my great desire by the grace of God is that everyone will experience the same.

If someone asks you, "Who is God and where to meet Him," what do you say?

The first thing I say to people is, God is love, and you meet God in true love. If you really want to meet Him personally, intimately in His complete presence, then you meet Him in the Eucharist which truly is the Body, Blood, Soul and Divinity of Our Lord, Jesus Christ. Every time I come to the Eucharist and receive Jesus I am filled with His divine love, His divine self, His divine joy. I am filled with what every other person can be filled with if they come seeking God where He is, in the Eucharist.

How did your travelling ministry begin?

The Lord asked me to go out, to go and spread His love. How can I refuse Him when I love Him? I would do anything for Him, anything except sin and of course He would never ask this. I asked Him, "How should I do this?" I didn't know. He replied, "Go and speak to your archbishop." I said, "The archbishop wouldn't speak to me, who am I? He has more important things to do than to speak to me!" The Lord said, "I will make it possible."

Then it happened through a priest I got to know. He invited me to a dinner he was having at the occasion of his 50 years' anniversary as a priest. The archbishop was there. The Lord said, "Go and ask him for an appointment." I was too nervous so I did not. However, God gave me another opportunity when a short time later the archbishop came and said Mass at a prayer group I attended. The Lord

17

said, "Speak to him." I asked, "How can I do it, so many will want to speak to him?" "I will bring him to you," the Lord replied. Then to my surprise the archbishop came right up to me and said, "Hello." So I asked for an appointment and I got to see him two or three days later. Before I saw him, I was in the cathedral praying and I was saying to the Lord, "What shall I do?"

He said, "Just open your mouth and I will give you all the words you should say to him." The Lord said, "Whatever the archbishop says to you, you must be totally obedient. If he tells you to be silent, not to go out to the world, you must do that. Trust in Me but remember always, you must be obedient to the Church." So I went in very nervously to the archbishop and I just started to explain to him how God had come into my life.

I was in there over an hour and at the end of this time, the archbishop gave me his support and his permission. He appointed a spiritual director to watch over me and for fourteen years now the archbishop has been supporting me. The spiritual director has been guiding me and checking everything I do to make sure nothing goes against Church teaching, that nothing is heretical, nothing goes against the love of God and in all this time, by God's grace, everything has been wonderful.

Trusting so much in the spiritual director, doesn't this mean putting God second place?

I believe everyone should have a spiritual director and that we should have a close relationship to priests because the priest is meant to be part of your family. When you have a spiritual director, a priest as your close friend, that is not putting the priest before Jesus. It is actually seeing Jesus in the priesthood. Also, you begin to understand what the priest is guiding you, telling you, is generally given by the Holy Spirit through the priest. That is a wonderful blessing of the priesthood, the great sacrament of the priesthood where the priest becomes Jesus to us. Where by the power of the Holy Spirit grace pours out through the priest to bless us and draw us closer to God. So it is very important that we listen to a priest and be obedient to a priest unless anything goes against faith and morals.

Would you rather rest at home sometimes?

I want to be at home and rest all the time. I have a beautiful wife whom I love very much, a real saint in the family and I miss her every day. However, if this was easy and if it wasn't a struggle ... and believe me, every day is a struggle ... then there wouldn't be much achieved. Jesus told me from the beginning, "It is never going to be easy, till the day you die, it is going to be a struggle." He said, "Look at My life, look at all the struggles I had, look what I had to endure, the cross I had to carry, the pain, the wounds, the suffering, the blood I shed, the heart I opened on the cross, the life I gave. If it was like that for Me, then do not expect it to be any easier for you. I will give you all the grace, all the strength, all the gifts you need if you only keep saying yes to My will."

I love Jesus so much, I can't say no to Him, I don't want to say no to Him. No matter how hard it gets, no matter what I have to give, I pray to God that I can continue to serve Him and please Him until my dying breath and beyond. But, it is hard for every Catholic, isn't it? If you try to live your faith, the world prepares many crosses for you.

Many people today are far away from God

Yes, people today seem to be far away from God because the world draws them away. It is very easy to be distracted and seduced by the world, by money, the excitement, all the things that seem so attractive. Usually the ways of the world are not the ways of God and the ways of the world bring a false happiness, a happiness that doesn't last. Many people know this because in their life they have some misery and unhappiness. They feel insecure, unloved, unwanted, so many difficulties in life.

So often these difficulties come because people have been drawn away from God by the evil one using the ways of the world to seduce people. Of course, when you turn to the world and to self, you welcome the embrace of evil even though you may not understand it.

When you embrace sin, all it brings is pain, hurt and suffering, sometimes it begins in small ways that usually grow and grow to cause great turmoil. We can see that in society today. So many families falling apart, marriages falling apart, so many people involved in drugs, alcohol and immorality. All this is because evil has seduced people through the world. Yet, there is God who is always reaching out to us, offering us goodness and happiness in this life, offering a love that will bring fullness of life. A love that will bring everything we need to us in life, but foolishly most people do not believe this or ignore this or are blind to it, just as I was.

I hope by the grace of God their eyes will be opened to see the emptiness in the world and to see the greatness, the fullness of God's love and what He offers us – eternal happiness, eternal life with Him. That eternal joy can begin in the moment you decide to embrace Jesus fully. God offers us that joy in every moment of our life on earth, true joy that will remain with us always. Sadly today, so many people deny themselves this and instead embrace the misery of the world.

How can their eyes be opened?

Many people, like me, do not even think of God even though, deep inside I knew that many of the things that I did were wrong and I was ashamed of them, I had little or no thoughts of God. Like I was, many people today just wander around thinking of self with no or few thoughts about God. As I looked back at my life I wondered why I had the experiences with heaven as I was certainly not looking for them. Later, the Lord explained to me that what happened to me was because of those people who are praying. Those people who are sacrificing in love for God and for others. Those people who are carrying crosses for Christ, Our Lord, and for other people, living their faith as best as they can, so often struggling and wondering, is anything happening because of it? Not realising through them and through their efforts to live that faith, God is pouring grace throughout the world, a grace that touched me and changed me and a grace that has touched and will touch many people.

I have met so many who said they were not even thinking of God but then, one day, they were opened to Him and they do not know how it happened. It happened through all those wonderful people who are living their faith and the grace of God poured out through them. So people should never feel they are not achieving anything, as they live their faith and nothing seems to happen. They should believe and understand because of their faith many people are being touched and changed.

So how can people's eyes be opened to God? They can be opened by the people of faith living their faith in prayer, in the sacraments, in obedience to the Church and by going out and showing the love of Christ to everyone they meet, unafraid of what the world might do to them. Knowing that as they reach out in Christ, Our Lord, that Our Lord is reaching out through them to touch many people. People that they may not see or know on this earth but they will know in heaven as all these people will come and thank them for the sacrifices they have made.

So people help save each other. That means your gifts are not for your life but for saving others?

The graces the Lord gave to me, He actually didn't give to me, they are graces that pass through me. Any graces or gifts are not mine, they are all of mankind's from God. Also, by sharing those graces and gifts that God pours out I receive the wonderful grace from Him to grow to know His love more and more. The gift He gives to me as I share the gifts and graces, is to let me experience His love deep inside in a wonderful way.

This grace is there for everyone who would share the gifts and graces God gives them. However, today, because of the ways of the world, many people think that the gifts and graces that they have, whether it is spiritual, physical or mental, are *their* gifts to benefit from so they can have a better life or more money or get more respect from people. How foolish that is because people have let evil work on their pride, a pride that stops them sharing what God gives. When they do not share as they are supposed to, the gifts and graces never grow and the world suffers, for the gifts are not being shared as they are meant to be.

So many gifted people – and when I say gifted people I mean everyone because we are all gifted in different ways, we are all graced in different ways, we are all gifts from God and we are all graced by God. Unfortunately today many people do not believe this or do not accept this. So they do not allow the gifts and the graces to reach their fullness for the benefit of all mankind. How satan laughs at our foolish pride. How ashamed so many of us are going to be on judgement day when Our Lord and Saviour asks of us why we did not use our gifts and graces for the good of all.

Do you find that people only see you as someone who could help them get a miracle?

I do not care why they come to see me. The important thing is that they come because when they come, God pours out His Holy Spirit to touch them in the way that is best for them. When Our Lord walked the earth, many people came to Him because of the miracles. Some did not come because of His word but because of the healings. So if that was good enough for Him, it is good enough for me.

What is your special charism?

God explained to me that by our baptism, every Catholic is charismatic. That the more we turn to God and accept His love into our life, the more every person is opened to his or her charisms. It is through the sacraments and through prayer and through obedience to God that we can be open wide to many charisms. The charisms God has given me are many because the greatest gift He gives me is His love and in that love is every charism that is needed.

So if the gift of healing is needed to bring people back to God, He gives me the gift of healing. If the gift of evangelisation is needed to bring people back, that is what He gives. Whatever gift is needed, He gives when it is needed at the time it is needed. The wonderful thing is that He offers the charisms to every Catholic. All we have to do to receive them is bow totally to His will, give ourselves totally to Him and live completely for Him. Then if we do this Jesus Christ, Our Lord, will pour His divine Holy Spirit deep inside us and give us every charism we need in every moment.

Could you explain more about the gift of healing?

There are many healed as God expresses the gift of healing through me. There have been thousands of healings. I see the healings as gifts of God that are given through the sacraments as wherever there is a healing service, of course, we have Holy Mass and there are priests hearing confessions. The healing comes through the Eucharist, the most powerful healing prayer of all and through confession where a healing of soul can occur with a complete and true confession. All this happens through the powerful sacrament of the priesthood through which God pours out His Divine grace. My talk and healing prayers just complement the sacraments.

I believe totally in that sacramental power of God. When I pray for people, I never ask for anything except that God will heal them in the way that is best for them. Sometimes people come up asking, can you ask God to heal me from cancer, or heal my bad leg, or my brain tumour? All I ever say to them is, "I will pray for you." All I pray for is that the best will happen for that person and then I leave it totally up to Our Lord and Saviour, knowing that He will do what is best. He knows what is best for us. So I trust totally in Him that He will do what is best for us. He always does, He never lets me down, sadly at times I let Him down.

Could you tell us about some healings that you found amazing?

There have been thousands and they all surprise me but I would like to share a couple of healings that are special to me. I was in South Africa in Johannesburg in a house for children with Aids where Mother Teresa's sisters work. There was a young boy who was about 18 months old. He was born with Aids and from the moment he was born he never stopped crying because he was in constant pain. He couldn't walk because his bones would break and he hardly ever slept because of the agony. It broke my heart to see this boy. I prayed with him just for a few seconds and my beautiful wife picked him up and her tears dropped on him and I think it is probably through these tears of love that God worked, not my prayers. But from that moment, he stopped crying. His pain stopped. When we went back the following year, they said he no longer had Aids. His bones would no longer break and he was running around healthy, laughing and smiling and I just felt so humble. How powerful the love of God is for little children.

Just one more that I would like to share with you. I was in Kenya and there was a young boy there about nine years old. He had been deaf since birth and came from a very poor family. His father had just died two weeks before and the boy was very depressed. I prayed with him just for a second and all of a sudden, he could hear. He was so happy and so were all of the nuns who were there. Later, when I was talking to them, they told me throughout his life he never really had joy and now this healing from God had really brought the first joy in his life and I thank God for that.

On my website (www.alanames.org), there are video clips showing two news reports from the USA. One is about a woman called Linda O'Rear who was in a wheel chair for many years. She had an immune problem as well and the doctors could not heal her. She came to one of my talks, I prayed with her just for a couple of seconds and God healed her immediately, she no longer needed a wheel chair nor the braces on the legs, and all her immune disease was cured. It was so spectacular that one of the television stations did a report on her.

Also, about three years ago, it was in the same town, San Antonio in Texas, there was a young boy who had one leg shorter than the other. It was about four inches shorter than the other leg. I prayed with him just for one or two seconds, and his short leg grew to be the same length as the other. That is the power of God's love. Again, it was so spectacular that a television station did a report.

God's love is so powerful He can heal anything and He wants to heal everyone. All He asks is that people come to Him with an open heart accepting His love and grace within, try to live as best they can to His way and He will heal them in the way that is best for them.

How do we open our heart to God?

Often people do ask me this question, how do we open our heart to God? The first thing you do, turn to God, turn to the Holy Spirit and say, "Lord, I can't do this myself, You help me to open my heart completely to You." Do not expect this to happen straight away but you have to persevere in this prayer and that perseverance is a powerful prayer in itself. The more and more you pray and ask the Holy Spirit to help you do this, slowly but surely your heart will start to open more and more to God and one day you will get a special touch of the love of God in your heart and then you will know that perseverance was all worthwhile.

Who is Mary for you?

She is my mother! She speaks to me just like a mother, always with love, always welcoming and always directing me to a better life, a holy life, directing me to God. Even in my physical life, she helps me. Once when I was a little bit overweight, she said to me, "Eat less and exercise more." Just as a mother would.

What is the Catholic Church for you?

The Catholic Church for me and hopefully for everyone in the Church is the Body of Christ, is the mystical Body of Christ where Jesus calls us into His mystical Body so that we can be one with Him. Where in that oneness with God we can find a full, a happy, a complete life. The Catholic faith is what Jesus gave to us and what He continues to give to us in the giving of Himself. So if we come to the Church and give ourselves to Christ in the Church, then we find the fullness of life that

He talked about. So for me the Catholic faith, the Catholic Church is everything because it is the Body of Christ.

Have you always been Catholic? And what was or is your profession?

I was baptised a Catholic but I never lived the faith. My mother is a strong Irish Catholic but I never listened to what she said. I had no faith at all. The only time I went to church, other than to steal from it, was once a year at Easter. I would go to communion and confession at Easter doing the yearly duty to remain Catholic because I thought all Catholics go to heaven. So I would do this once a year insurance policy so that if heaven existed I would go there but it did not mean anything.

My work ... I used to be a sales manager of a pharmaceutical company which was a high paying job. However, the moment God came into my life and He asked me, would I work for Him, I knew I could no longer do that job. It was about 18 months or two years after God started speaking to me, with my wife's agreement, we decided to commit ourselves totally to God. So my work now is only working for God in the Catholic Church. So all I do is evangelise and pray with people and I write books as well.

Many youth are in the same situation as you described before. They are baptised but don't know how to live the faith. What is your advice for them to live their faith?

Every day, they should think about how they are living and see how, as I found, when I lived the way of the world, I never felt truly happy. I never felt truly fulfilled, I never felt truly loved, I had so much insecurity, so much anger and so much bitterness at times. Life was so miserable. Life is not meant to be like that!

If you live the way of the world and seek excitement in the ways of the world, then most people are going to end up with those bad feelings, with this miserable life. However, if you turn to Jesus, He brings excitement into your life. He lifts you beyond this world. He gives you what no drugs, no alcohol, no free sex can give you.

With all these things, the excitement only lasts a short while and then it disappears but the excitement that Jesus brings lasts forever and it grows and grows. Always, when you embrace Him, you have a peace inside, always you feel loved. You never feel unwanted, you don't feel afraid. Life becomes joyful, becomes happy, as it is meant to be. Everyone has a choice, a choice that God has given us from the very beginning. He says, "Live My way and be happy. If you do not want to live My way, well, then you are going to be unhappy." I encourage everyone, try and live the way of God.

I know it will be hard but the important thing is to try and to keep asking God to help you in your trying. If you make the effort, even though you may make mistakes and fall, through all your weaknesses, God will pour His grace into you and you will find joy and happiness. So I encourage people, do not make the foolish choices that I made in the past, the choices that lead you into evil which only brings pain, hurt and suffering into your life because that is what evil does. Make the choice of goodness, make the choice of God, make the choice of Jesus Christ. Make the right choice and have a good and happy life.

The following are excerpts from talks by Alan Ames, given and recorded in several countries including Germany, Austria, Switzerland, Italy, Spain, the United States and others.

I came from a very poor family and grew up in London. My father was a violent alcoholic gambler. The money he didn't drink he gambled away. So often we did not even have food. Due to this, I had become angry with the world, and through my anger, the evil one reached into my life and blinded me to the love of God. When I looked at other families and saw all the things they had, I thought, "How could a God exist that He would let some people have lots of things and others have nothing. If there is a God, He cannot let this happen." So I decided at a very early age that God did not exist.

I thought the only one who would look after me was myself. I must tell you that my father had a very big conversion before he died few years ago. Anyway, I began to live a life of sin. I became jealous of just about everyone and decided that I would get what I wanted in life, regardless of what it cost. To get what I wanted, I would just steal, cheat, swindle, do anything to get things of the world. I was very successful in doing so. In imitation of my father, I also became an alcoholic. As I got older, I became a member of a motorcycle gang, I became very violent and addicted to many things. The only time I would think about God was when I got into trouble and I might say,

"God help me!" I migrated to Australia and found that Australians are heavy drinkers so I fitted in really well.

The more I drank, the more violent I got and life got worse and worse. I would fight just about anyone. It was a bad life for my family because sometimes I would go out and drink for ten or twelve hours, come home, say unkind things to my wife and my children and then go out drinking again. So it wasn't very good for them. I think it was only by the grace of God that they put up with me. Life went on like that, getting worse and worse.

Dreams

One day, I started to have dreams about disasters and people dying and they all happened, they all died just as I had dreamt. I could not believe it. It was all sorts of people. It started to get really frightening. So many bad dreams and they always happened, they always came true. This started to concern me a little bit. I was getting frightened to sleep at night because I was frequently having these dreams and within a couple of days, the disasters would happen or the people would die. Sleep was not easy at that time. Then I began to drink more and more. I was drinking enough as it was, but now I was drinking more so as to get some sleep at times but that did not stop the dreams, they carried on.

With one of the disasters I experienced, I was in a plane that crashed into a block of flats and I saw the people around me die; children and adults. Two days later, it was on the news that a plane crashed into a block of flats in Belgium. It was exactly as I saw it. It was pretty terrifying at that time and my wife was very scared because I would wake up in the middle of the night, sometimes screaming and shouting and it frightened her. Life was going on like that and it got worse and the dreams were getting more graphic and many terrible things happened. I did not think about God that time. I just thought, "Maybe they will go away." But they didn't.

It was really getting bad when one day a man appeared and began to strangle me, there was nothing I could do to stop him. When I tried to hold on to him or strike him my hands went through him. I thought I was going to die. Then a voice started speaking to me. The voice said to pray the 'Our Father,' which in desperation I did, as soon as I began to pray the strangling stopped. This voice said it was an angel and that God had sent the angel to me because He loved me and He wanted my love and He wanted to help me. I tried not to listen to the angel at first as I didn't believe in angels, I thought they do not

31

exist. They are like fairies, they are not real. So I asked the angel to prove it was real.

Then the angel started to tell me things that would happen in my life. I was really surprised because they all happened. Now even with the angel telling me that the angel loved me and God loved me and that I should change my life and turn to God and these bad things would stop, I didn't take any notice. I just carried on drinking, carried on fighting, did all the bad things I was doing and the bad dreams carried on.

One day when I was travelling for work, I was in a city called Adelaide, which is about 2000 km from where I live. It was about nine o'clock at night and I was in a hotel room there and the angel said to me, "I will have to leave you because you have not changed. You are just the same as when I first came to you. You are no different." This was so true. Suddenly the angel was gone. I felt really sad because through all these bad things, the turmoil that was happening in my life at that time, there was this soft gentle voice talking about love and now it was gone.

Saint Teresa and the rosary

However, very quickly another voice started speaking to me. It was a female voice and it was very strict, very stern. She said to me, "If you don't change your life, you are going to hell. You have got to stop drinking, you have got to stop fighting, you have got to start loving God and fellow man, and you have got to start praying the rosary three times a day." She said, "Look at all the bad things happening in your life now. This is because you have turned to sin and you are allowing evil into your life. If you turn to God, this will go from you. Your life will become a joy, not a misery as it is at the moment. You are making a free choice to accept sin in your life and you are allowing these things to happen."

She said, "When you drink, you open yourself up to evil." This was because I was drinking so much with no control. I was just opening myself up and allowing evil to touch me. She said, "If you do not change, you are going to hell, and by your free choice." She was very hard on me like an old school teacher telling me off. She said she was Saint Teresa of Avila. That meant nothing to me. I only knew Saint Patrick because mum is Irish, Saint George because I was born in England and a couple of the apostles I had heard of.

Anyway, Saint Teresa was telling me off saying, "Pray the rosary, pray the rosary. You have got to start praying. You have got to come closer to God. Prayer and the sacraments are the only way." I didn't have a rosary. I had only prayed it maybe two or three times in my life when my mum had forced me to do it (except once when I was on holiday in Ireland at age fifteen and I was very sick. As I slipped into a coma and nearly died I was for some unknown reason praying the rosary as I became unconscious). So I used that as an excuse. I told her, "I don't have a rosary, I can't pray it." I thought that would get me out of it but I was wrong.

She said, "There is a shop around the corner that is open and if you go there, it sells rosaries." I thought, "At nine o'clock at night, you don't get any shop to open at this time!" But she kept insisting, "Go there and get a rosary." So off I went. The shop was there, it was open and it sold rosaries. I went inside, and she directed me to a brown one. Later I discovered it was the colour of the order she belonged to.

I went back to the hotel room with the rosary in my hand and I started all the real excuses then. "This is boring! I don't want to pray this! Real men don't pray! I want to go down to the pub and have some beer. I don't want to waste my time saying all these 'Our Father's' and 'Hail Mary's.' I can't even remember how to pray the rosary," but she kept insisting.

She said, "I will be your teacher, I will teach you." Finally, with her more than gentle persuasion, as she is very direct and very strict, I gave in. I started to pray the rosary. To my surprise from the first prayer, I got this calmness, a peace, a joy, a happiness within. Something I had not felt in my life before. I felt loved, so different and I didn't want to stop praying.

Then what happened at that time was the lights in the room were flickering on and off with a lot of noise from the doors and drawers moving. Normally, if something like that would have happened, I would have been terrified but by the grace of the Holy Spirit I didn't take much notice of it. Saint Teresa said, "Just ignore it. It is satan who wants to stop you from praying. He is trying to stop you coming back to God. Just keep praying and do not take any notice."

Saint Teresa kept encouraging me, "Pray, think about Jesus' life as you pray the rosary. You can trust completely in God. Have no fear, just trust in God. Give everything to Him. There is nothing the other one can do to you. It is up to you. Now is the chance to change your life, to come back to God. You have been away from God and allowed satan to get hold of you. Now is the chance to open your heart and come back to God. You have to do that through a sacramental and prayerful life. There is no other way."

So I listened to what she said and I focused on Jesus and prayed the rosary, and within about five minutes, these noises stopped and they didn't come back. This showed me very early on not to pay evil any attention and to keep focusing on God because what evil wants is to distract us. He wants us to look to him, to look to the evil one, because when we are thinking of him and looking to him, we are not thinking about God.

As I am travelling around the world now I meet a lot of people who always seem to be talking about evil and about satan and all the bad things that are happening or may happen. They are focusing on this instead of focusing on God as they are meant to. I always try not to be drawn into that and to look straight to God.

I started praying the rosary fifteen decades a day from that moment, which truly was a miracle. I did so because I wanted those bad things to stop in my life and I was really enjoying prayer, feeling so peaceful. The more I prayed, the more I wanted to pray. These things still carried on but not to the same extent. They seemed to ease off for a while.

As time went on, I found prayer a little boring because I kept thinking about the same thing as I prayed the rosary. I just kept thinking about Jesus' life in one way. Saint Teresa said to me, "There are many ways to meditate in prayer. Do not trap yourself in one way. Because when you do, well, it will become tedious. It may be boring. The evil one will be working on that weakness that you have to make it more boring so that you will give up and won't pray anymore. That's what he wants."

She said, "When you pray, ask the Holy Spirit to guide you in your prayers. God never expects you to do anything by yourself. He calls you into a partnership with Him where He wants to help you. So in praying the rosary ask the Holy Spirit to help you think about how God the Father acted and felt throughout the life of Jesus. Or Our Blessed Mother, how she shared in His life, watching her Son grow before her. How she saw Him suffer and die, His resurrection … her feelings, her emotions. The apostles and women who followed Jesus, the Jews who opposed Him, the soldiers who crucified Him. Then you will find there will be many ways to meditate on the life of Jesus in the rosary."

As I did that and asked the Holy Spirit for the grace to lead me, many more ways opened up. I found it is an endless kaleidoscope on the life of Jesus in the rosary when you open up by the grace of the Holy Spirit, when He guides you. So do not be trapped in one way. Do not say the same meditation all the time and do not only think from the mind in your prayers. Let God guide you from your heart and He will show you many wonders, many joys in your prayer. Then you will find the happiness that is supposed to be in every word of every prayer.

Later Our Blessed Mother said, "This is what the rosary is. It is guiding you to look at my son, Jesus, His life on earth. To see His life here on earth, which leads us closer to Him and to let Him lead us to heaven. Always remember that when you pray the rosary."

The gift of joyful prayer and the Holy Spirit

Saint Teresa of Avila explained to me that prayer was meant to be a continuous focus to God. How, as you keep looking to God the Father, the Son and the Holy Spirit in your prayers, He opens your soul and lifts you to higher spiritual levels so that you can experience what a wonderful gift prayer is.

Sometimes when people pray, they have such long faces, they look so sad, so miserable. They look like they have the weight of the world on their shoulders. It is as if prayer is a heavy burden. It is no wonder that many of the young do not want to come to church as they see people in the church looking so unhappy.

Later Our Blessed Mother and the Lord Himself explained that many people have lost the joy of loving God in their prayers, that every word should be a joy, should be filled with happiness. This though only happens when you ask God for that grace, when you ask God to lead you, to open your heart so that you can receive that joy, that peace, that contentment, that happiness within you.

When you pray only from the mind, all you may do is put barriers of self between you and God and allow evil to distract you with so many different thoughts. It is then that your prayers can become a burden, a chore, a duty instead of the wonderful gift of love God gives us. In prayer is the grace to open our hearts and accept God's love within with each word of the prayer that we speak from our heart. Prayer is meant to be a joy, not a burden.

If it is a burden for you then it may be because you are not asking God to guide you in your prayers and you are not allowing Him to give you that wonderful gift that He wants to give to everyone. God will never force Himself upon you. He allows you to keep these barriers if you want to but He is waiting for your complete invitation to come and fill you with His love, joy and peace.

Prayer is meant to be joyful, happy, exciting. Often people do not experience that, as when they pray, they are thinking about themselves and not about God. Their focus is on the world, on their problems in life. When you pray you are supposed to look beyond self, beyond the world and look to God in heaven. When you do pray in that way, that is when God reaches out and takes hold of your very soul and lifts it deep into His heart. However, first you must keep your heart looking to God, not looking to self and to be able to do that you have to turn to the Holy Spirit asking for the grace to do so.

It is when you rely on yourself, you are bound to fail in your prayers because you are human, you are weak, you are fragile and evil will distract you. There will be so many thoughts flowing into your mind, distracting you from God. When you are looking away from God, your heart begins to close to him and that is what evil wants.

As you recognise your weakness and turn to the Holy Spirit and say, "Lord, help me to pray. Lead me in prayer so my heart, my very soul will open to You and You can pour Your divine grace inside." When you turn to the Holy Spirit in that way and ask for help, He gives it to you but you must keep asking, you can't expect it the first time, you must continuously ask. When you continuously seek the help of the Spirit of truth, the Spirit of love, the Spirit of God in anything, He answers your prayer.

As I came to experience this wonderful joy in prayer, I wanted everyone in the world to experience the same thing, because if they did, the world would be such a different place, full of happy, peaceful, loving people. That is what the grace of God turns people into.

Unfortunately so many people do not experience that. So many young people turn to drugs, to alcohol, to free sex and to so many other things, getting their false joy there. Yet this divine joy from God is there for every person. However, many Catholics do not experience this wonderful grace in prayer, this wonderful joy, and so many Catholics are not filled by the peace that comes with joy. So if we do not experience it, how can we expect the rest of the world to experience it? How can we expect the young people to come and seek God if they do not see His peace, His joy and His love in us?

That is why it is very important, when you pray or when you do anything, to first ask the Holy Spirit to help you open yourself completely to God. So that you in your life, in your heart, in your soul, can receive this wonderful grace and that the love of God can be poured out through you to attract others to Him.

A Trinitarian way of praying

With the terrible pride that I have as I was praying over time and experiencing so many graces, I thought, "Oh, I know everything about prayer." But the saints decided to show me that I did not. They showed me there are many more ways to pray and that all these different ways are there to open me to God. Our Blessed Mother, Mary, showed me a Trinitarian way of prayer.

She said, "There is another way to pray, one you should try. When you say the words of your prayers, at the same time think them and as you think them, pray them, express them from your heart and soul."

I tried to do that and somehow I could not do it. After a great struggle I finally managed to put my words and my thoughts together. I struggled for so long till I finally got it. However, I did not feel the joy I had in other prayers. I just could not get my heart and my soul into my prayers.

Then Our Lady explained, "You have forgotten something. You are not asking the Holy Spirit to help you pray from your heart and soul." I thought how stupid I was. So now I asked for the help of the Holy Spirit and after a short time, with perseverance, it was so different. As I prayed, my words, my thoughts and my heartbeats were united in each word. As I would say the word, I was thinking the word. As I was thinking the word, I was feeling the word deep inside me. All of a sudden, I could get my words, my thoughts and my heartbeats into each of my prayers. They became one, a total expression of my love for God. My entire being was in every word of each prayer. I felt the love of God filling me and embracing me and drawing me closer to Him and oh, I was lifted on high! It was wonderful.

In that way, in each prayer, I gave myself completely to God, all by the grace of God, because God loves me and He wanted me to experience His love in another way through prayer. When I prayed in that way, I could feel His love so powerfully because when I gave myself to Him in this prayer of total love, of total giving, He poured His love into me and surrounded me with His love. It was wonderful.

Our Blessed Mother explained, "Now you are praying completely, using your whole self in a Trinitarian way of praying. Physically, in your words, also in your mind and in your soul. As you pray in this way, your soul lifts your physical and your mental self to God. Your spirit cries out your love for Him, and then as you pray in this way, His divine Spirit comes deep inside you because now you are totally desiring Him, you are giving your total self to Him in prayer and in return, He gives you Himself."

Perseverance

Some time after saint Teresa had first taught me to pray, I asked her, "When I was praying it seemed like Jesus was stepping back or He was not there." Saint Teresa said, "What He was doing was, as He was stepping back, He was leading you forward. By your perseverance, by your continually focusing on Him, He was drawing you into higher levels of grace." She explained that many people call this the dry times and sadly in these dry times, often people look away from God instead of focusing harder on Him. As in those moments, if you keep your focus on Jesus, then you will take giant steps of grace.

God will lead you to higher and higher levels of grace and what happens as a result is the scales fall off your eyes. That is what happened to me. As I was praying and experiencing this wonderful joy, all of a sudden, the ways of the world became so obvious. I saw that the way I had been living in the past was the wrong way and I saw how I hurt God and so many people. I also saw the good way and saw that if I had lived that way, happiness, joy and peace would be mine.

Later on I was shown that through me living God's way, God will pour out His grace through me to touch others and to bring them the same peace, happiness and joy. The saints told me that if I wanted to continue praying in this way, to be led to higher levels of grace, that again I had to turn to the Holy Spirit because in my self, I am weak, I am human, I am fragile. If I rely on myself, I am bound to fail but if I turn to the Holy Spirit and say, "Lord, help me, help me pray properly," then the Holy Spirit will reach out and lead me deeper into prayer.

As I was given this sort of spiritual sight, I was also shown by the Holy Spirit that I need to ask His help in everything. When I come to the sacraments, I have to turn to the Holy Spirit and ask Him to help me celebrate them properly. When I read Holy Scripture, I must do the same.

From then on when I began to pray, the Holy Spirit was taking hold of me and keeping my focus on heaven. Due to that, my heart and my soul, were opened in love to God and He poured His grace inside. This can be experienced by every person if, when they begin to pray, they first ask the Holy Spirit for help. Do not expect this to happen straight away. You will have to persevere. For some reason, it happened straight away to me but most people have to persevere before they experience this. The Holy Spirit explained later that this perseverance is a special prayer in itself because it shows the depth of your love for God and how much you want His love.

Through this perseverance, God pours out many graces. Often they are graces you do not see because as you struggle, persevere and carry your crosses, as you try and focus on heaven, through you the Holy Spirit pours out graces for the world. That is how people like me are changed unexpectedly, it is by others' sacrifices and perseverance and the grace God gives through their perseverance of love.

Making every moment a prayer

Our Blessed Mother said to me that I should try to make every day a prayer because I was now experiencing so much joy in prayer and I wanted to have this joy in every moment. She said I could achieve this by making every second of the day a prayer of love to God.

Our Blessed Mother also encouraged me to live every second in the way of Jesus. She said, "If you want a full and happy life, if you want to walk away from evil in your life and walk towards goodness, imitate my son Jesus. He came to earth to show mankind how to live. He gave mankind a clear map on how to reach heaven." She explained to me, "You must try and live every second of every day the way of Jesus. That every thought you have, every word you speak, you should make a prayer of love to the Father, just as Jesus did." I thought to myself, "That is really hard, I do not think I can do that." Our Blessed Mother said, "In yourself, you cannot do that but if you turn to the Holy Spirit and ask for His help, He will help you do it. So make your first prayer every day one to the Holy Spirit, asking Him to keep your focus on heaven in all you do, asking Him to make every step you take a step following Jesus." So I started to do that and things were much easier, but it is still hard, because living the way of Christ is not easy but by God's grace I persevere.

When I tried to live in love always at first, nothing seemed to happen. It was really difficult to do. This was because I had forgotten to ask the Holy Spirit to help me. Then Our Blessed Mother said, "You are trying to do it by yourself. God has never asked you to do things alone. From the beginning, He has called mankind to a partnership of love where He wants to help you in everything you do. He is just there for you. So remember to ask the Holy Spirit to help you." So I began to do that, and then it changed. Now I seem to be able to offer every moment of the day to God. Every thought I have, every word I speak, every action I do, every breath I take, every heartbeat now becomes a prayer of love to God and all because I asked God to help me.

In every day, I can see the love that God gives us. In creation all around us, in the air I feel God's love touching me. When there is a breeze, I feel the Lord kissing me on the cheek. When I look upon another and see them smile, I see Jesus smiling at me. In the animals I see the wonder of God's love. Now all around me, I see and experience God's love each day and it is wonderful.

When I breathe in at times, I breathe in, in thanks to God for the gift He gives me with each breath. When I breathe out I ask God to pour His divine grace out in every breath to touch the world. I thank

God that I am breathing this same air that Jesus, that God, breathed. Every time I feel my heartbeat, I feel a touch of God in my very being as I realise that every heartbeat is a gift from God, a gift of His love, that by His grace I can return to Him in love.

Every day as I look at people, I see Jesus in them. Now when I see the sun, the sky, the animals, I see God's grace in them and I can't stop thanking God for those wonderful gifts. All day long, no matter what happens, no matter how much I am distracted, inside me I feel this burning love of God and I feel my heart calling out my love for Him.

As I started to pray in this way, every day became a prayer. Yes, I still struggle at times. Sometimes I forget to make that offering. Sometimes I fall down when the crosses are so heavy, but always the Holy Spirit is there encouraging me and helping me, saying, "Do your best, that is all I expect." The Holy Spirit has helped me and continues to help me overcome all the difficulties, as He will help anyone who asks with a true heart. At times when the crosses are so heavy I do not think I can go on. When I fall down and think, I cannot get up again, when the cross feels so heavy and I say, "Lord, I cannot do this anymore," the Holy Spirit fills me with His grace, with His power, He lifts me up and helps me to persevere. Then I know that with Him, anything good is possible and that nothing can stop me from loving God in each moment because God gives me the power to do so if I ask Him. The wonderful thing is He will give it to every person because He loves us all the same and He wants all of us to love Him the same, completely, in every moment.

My first prayer every morning when I open my eyes is to the Holy Spirit, asking Him to help me offer every second of the day as a prayer of love to God. Every word I speak, every thought I have, every action I do, every breath I take, every heartbeat now, by the grace of God, becomes a prayer of love to God. He helps me over and over and yes, I still fall down at times, I still make so many mistakes. Sometimes I think I have got to be a complete idiot because every day I sin, I cannot help it. I have bad thoughts, I say stupid things, and I am sure if most of you good people had happen to you what was happening in my life, you would be so holy, you would be saints. But every day I stumble, I fall down. However, every time I fall down I ask the Holy

Spirit to help me, and He does. He takes my focus from self and from the world and brings it back onto God. So now, every stumble, every fall, becomes a special prayer of love where I can offer my weaknesses to God in love.

If we ask the Holy Spirit to help us, He gives us the sight we need to live in the right way. He fills us with peace, with joy, with happiness in every moment and the Holy Spirit shines brightly into our soul. For this to happen, every day every person needs to commit themselves completely to God and not commit themselves to the world.

Turn to the Holy Spirit and say, "Lord, fill me with the grace I need, fill me with the strength I need, lead me along the path of Jesus Christ, so I can live His way and in Him find a full and happy life." It is when you do that, not only do you find fullness of life, but so do those around you, your family, your friends. Because what happens is: As you are filled with the Holy Spirit, as you give yourself to Him in each day, He pours the grace out through you to touch those around you and draw them closer to Him. His grace is magnified through you to bring peace to the world. For this to happen all it needs is for you to say yes to that peace in your heart, in your soul, every day.

Trust in God

As I try to offer every moment as a prayer of love to God, I am opened to receive His grace in every moment of the day and His peace fills me in each moment. In each moment I feel God's love. I feel His presence, I feel it filling me and I know He is always there to lift me up and to help me on, to care for me and protect me as He does for every person.

I was in the Holy Land a couple of years ago and the Lord showed me how He protects me and cares for me and how there is nothing to fear if you live for God. I was giving a talk in a town called Ramallah in the West Bank. The week before, the Muslims had been killing Christians. They had gone into Catholic and Greek Orthodox houses, pulling the men out and killing them. They had killed about twenty men that week. When I gave my talk, some Muslims came along which I thought was a great blessing.

Anyway, afterwards I was sitting in the priest's house and having a meal with him when there was a knock on the door. The housekeeper went to open the door and she came running into the room where we were with a look of fear on her face. She said nervously, "There is a group of Muslim men outside and they want Alan Ames." The priest said to me, "Do not go." My wife was with me and I said to her, "I have to go. This is what God calls me to." In her love of God she agreed.

As I stood up I could feel God around me and I could feel Him filling me and I knew He never lets me down. But I have to tell you, when I put my hand on the door to open it and step outside, I wondered if that would be my last moment. So I said, "Lord, if it is my last moment, it is Yours." Living for Him every moment had taken all fear away and the desire only to please Him and to do His will. So I opened the door and went outside and there was a big group of young Muslim men. One came forward and asked, "Are you Alan Ames?" I replied, "Yes, I am." They said, "Our friend has cancer, would you pray for him?" So I did.

Once again God showed me there is nothing to fear in life if you live every day for Him as a prayer of love for Him. That He will use you even in the most unusual conditions to touch others with His love. This is what every Catholic is meant to do. Not to be afraid, but to live each moment, each day as a prayer of love for God. Going out to others unafraid sharing His love. That's what God called the apostles to do and they said yes, and the results were miraculous. God calls us to do the same and if we do, the results through us will also be miraculous.

Bowing to God's will

As I started offering every moment of my life as a prayer of love to God, my whole day changed. Every moment, even the most difficult moment now is full of peace and love. Inside me now every moment is exciting because I know that moment is offered to God and accepted by God. Now every moment is a treasure that God fills with His grace. Now every moment I can show my love of God because I give every moment to Him, bowing totally to His divine will.

What happened as I started to do this and continue trying to do this, not only did my life change for the better but also the people around me. Now peace and happiness seemed to touch my wife, my children and some of my friends. Our Lord later said, "This is the way it works. When a person bows to My will and gives themselves totally to Me, then I fill that person with My grace and then that grace pours out through them to touch all those around. They become a light burning brightly in the dark and as that divine light pours out through them, it touches others and sets fire to others and then they again touch others and set fire to them. This is how the world will be changed for the better."

When those who love Him, when those who seek His love bow down before Him every day and say, "Here I am; Lord, do whatever You want with me, use me in whatever way You want." When you do that and mean that, now you are sacrificing your life for God just as God sacrificed His life for you and now in that sacrificial life, God pours out power, grace and mercy through you. All it takes is you saying your yes every day, and believe me if you do, your life will change for the better.

Learning how to discern

Heaven asked me to go to Holy Mass more. I was a once-a-year-man. I would go at Easter to receive Communion and confession, just in case the Catholic faith was true. If it was, I was a Catholic and if I died, I would go to heaven. It was an insurance policy. But now I started going to Mass once a week, twice a week, three times a week; confession once a month. I felt so saintly, I really felt holy. But still I didn't understand how far from God I truly was.

In the past, Mass meant nothing to me, but all of a sudden now it was so important. I could see the love of Jesus, of the Father and of the Holy Spirit in the Mass. I could see the sacrifice of Jesus in the Mass, how much He gave for us. I felt at times that I was at the Last Supper with Jesus, and all of a sudden, I wanted to go to Mass more and more. Now I go every day and it is wonderful, it truly is.

As I went into church, I was looking at the statues and they started to come alive. I would start to see different angels and different saints. They would always be saying the same things to me but in different ways.

The message was, "If you want to come closer to God, you must receive the sacraments, you must pray, you must read Holy Scripture." They said there is no other way. The saints said, today, there are many other ways suggested but they are all wrong. If they do not focus on prayer, the sacraments and Holy Scripture, they are wrong. They take you from God instead of to God. The angels and saints explained that many good sounding messages or so-called good messages are given. But often they focus on the person's rights, the person's self, what's good for them and their family, looking after themselves. There might be a slight mention of God, but usually the focus is on self, to take you away from God, to take you away from what's good for you, your future, your life. They are all self, self, self.

— *False messages*

Satan makes his messages look attractive, as if they were messages of love, there to help everyone, but they always have wrongs in them. Little wrongs that are there to take you from God.

Things like, "You can do what you want as long as it doesn't hurt anyone else." But when you do what you want, eventually you are bound to hurt someone else and you are bound to hurt yourself because you are not doing what God wants. You must focus on God in your life and not on self. It is when you focus on self, you start to close your heart to God and you start to step away from Him.

The angels and saints were always there encouraging me, helping me especially in the difficult times. However, at times in the beginning, I was tricked because I would be looking to the statues and often I would see angels and saints but sometimes when I was seeing them, they looked a little bit different. They did not have a nice expression on their face, let's put it that way. I did not realise that satan could imitate angels and saints and Our Lady and Our Lord but he can and he tricked me occasionally in the beginning. What would happen, he would start to speak to me and it sounded really nice. Then all of a sudden, there would be something in it that made me feel uncomfortable, something would not seem right.

Later, Jesus explained to me that satan is so clever. What the evil one does is, he gives many good messages because he can do that. However, what he does is put one or two lines in them that are wrong so the whole message seems right, but there is a little bit in it that is wrong, and that little bit leads you away from God. Then the next time, he puts a little bit more in it and this leads you further away from God. You have to be so careful.

Jesus said to me, "If someone wanted to counterfeit a 20-Dollar-note, he would make it as close as possible to a 20-Dollar-note so that people would accept it. If it would look different, people would not accept it, would they? This is what satan does when he wants to trick you. He makes the messages look so close to God's messages so that they look okay. But what he does, he puts a little wrong in there, and it is that little wrong that takes you away from God. Then you accept a bigger wrong and a bigger wrong, and all of a sudden, you are so far from God."

One of the things Our Blessed Mother and Jesus said to me is, "Always, in every message you receive, make sure it leads you to a sacramental and a prayerful life. Make sure whoever gives the message accepts the presence of Our Lord, Jesus, in the Eucharist, the Body and Blood of Jesus, and meditate on that whenever you see or hear something, and then satan will find it more difficult to trick you."

It was very hard in the beginning but as I did what Our Lord said and what Our Lady said, I found satan could not stay there, he just disappeared because he is so frightened of the presence of Our Lord.

It seems so many of us are frightened of evil and we should not be. So many of us have fear, we are so worried and concerned what he could do in our life. When we have these fears and these concerns, we somehow open a little gate for him to come in and to annoy us and frustrate us. If you can, let go of these fears and worries and trust in God the gate will remain closed to evil. It is when you have these fears there is an eroding of your trust in God. It is you saying, "Maybe satan can do something to me, maybe God is not strong enough to look after me."

The truth is that God is far stronger than the evil one. God's strength is insurmountable. If you trust in God completely, you shall have no fear at all of evil for you know God will look after you, He will take care of you. He has promised He will. It is up to you to accept that and to trust in that.

Fears and death

I was fortunate in one way, because the Lord was showing me and teaching me. There were so many bad things happening in my life at that time, even though there were many good things but it seemed the more the good things happen, the harder the bad ones get.

— *The fear of death*

What started to happen over a period of time was I started to get physical attacks from satan or evil ones which in the beginning I was very frightened of and concerned about. With some I thought I was going to die, someone would attack me and there was nothing I could do to stop them physically. However, every time this happened, a thought came to my mind, words came saying, "Think of Jesus, think of Jesus!"

Every time I did that and every time I said, "Jesus, if it is Your will that I die now, I give You my soul." Every time I said that, the attack stopped and evil went.

I was on a plane once, coming back from Sydney, which is the main city in Australia, to Perth where I live. We were half way back when one of the engines blew up. There were flames everywhere. The lights went out in the plane, there were fumes in the plane, and there was panic because of the thought we were going to crash. I was praying the rosary at that time and I just said to Jesus, "Lord, if we are going to die now, take us all to heaven. If it is Your will that we die, take us to heaven." Then I saw Jesus put His hand under the plane and hold us up. Our Lady put her arms around the plane and embraced it.

As they did that, the lights came on, we flew for one and a half hours on one engine and made it safely to Adelaide where everyone cheered when we landed. Again, the Lord showed me if you trust completely in Him and give yourself completely to Him, there is nothing the evil one can do to you. There is nothing to be frightened of. When that happened on that plane and at other times when you think you would be frightened, I was surprised that I was not frightened. In the past, I used to be so afraid of dying. This used to be a big fear in my life.

I know there are some among you here that are frightened of dying and so worried about it, but there is no need to be. Who here is not going to die, raise your hand! Death is part of life and it is not to be feared. We are only afraid of death because we have allowed evil to work on us to make us afraid of this gift of death. The gift that opens us completely to the Lord and allows Him to lift us into Him, into His eternal love, His eternal bliss where we can remain with Him forever in that divine joy. So why are we afraid? If you live in Jesus you would see that in Him, death leads to heaven. When we give our lives to Him and die in Him, then He resurrects us to the new life in heaven. So we should not be afraid of death, yet so many are. It shows they truly do not believe in the victory of Christ over death. It shows that they truly do not believe in the life, death and resurrection of Jesus and the promise He has given that He will bring us to eternal life with Him.

In every Eucharist there is the victory of Our Lord, Jesus, over evil. It is when we come to Jesus in the Eucharist and say, "Lord, let me die to myself and come to life in You in this victory," then God lifts us up on the cross with Him, helping us die to self. He then resurrects you in Him and fills you with the power of His victory. Now you know there is nothing to fear. You are afraid of nothing because you know your life is in God's hands and you will only die when He wants you to. When you live totally in the Eucharist, all your fears fall away. In the Eucharist you see the life, the death, the resurrection of Jesus and you experience it and you know it is true. Then truly, you know the love of God. You know God loves you, He will take care of you, He will look after you and you never fear again and you never worry again. The fear of death just disappears because you know that the moment of death is a blessed moment not a cursed one.

It seems so many people want to live to 100 or 150, searching to live forever. How foolish that is! If you live to 150, you will have to work until you are 148. Who wants to do that? When you love Jesus, you do not want to cling on to this life. You treasure this life for the wonderful gift that it is but you know it is not everything. It is just a moment in eternity. A blink of an eye, and you know in the life to come is everything. In Christ, Our Lord, death is a wonderful gift because the faithful in death come to embrace Christ, Our Lord, in love, to be drawn into eternal love, to share that love with Him forever. When you take your last breath He is waiting there for you to embrace you and to take you to heaven. So why should we fear death?

Fear should not be part of your life, fear should only reside with evil, not with us, the victors in Christ, Our Lord. We should be afraid of nothing because if we live in the love of God, we have nothing to fear and everything to hope for.

— *The joy in death*
I used to think, "When you go, you are being put into a box and put in the ground and that's the end of it." It is not that at all! There is so much God offers us after death. Death is a gift to all of us, a special gift if we embrace it in God's love. It is not seen as a gift when we become frightened, when we become fearful, when we allow satan to put these doubts in our mind.

If we can understand that heaven does exist and if we trust in Jesus that this is where we will go, we should have no fear of death. Death is a special grace for all of us. A mother of a friend died and she was a good friend to me as well, and I went to her funeral. Everyone there was so sad and crying, and yet I was so happy. I was so happy for her because I knew she has gone to God. What a wonderful gift He has given to that woman and I felt so joyful inside. I wondered why was everyone else so sad? Yes, she has left them behind, they are going to miss her but she has gone to God, we should be happy.

One of the things Christians have lost is the joy in death that God offers us as a special gift. So many of us are so upset when someone we know dies. So frightened when someone dies, so worried. Some day we are going to die and we should not worry, there is nothing to be frightened of. Death comes to all of us, it is like birth. Jesus offers us eternal life and death is the step to that eternal life, to eternal love. If you live your life on earth close to Jesus, in His love, in His arms, then there is nothing to be frightened of.

Understand where that fear comes from. It is coming from the evil one. He is trying to get these doubts into your mind, put these fears there so that maybe you turn from God and turn to other things in the hope for some other sort of life. But there is only one true life to come and that is in Jesus. Everything else is false. Everything else is a trick. So please, do not be frightened of death, just welcome it when it comes. Do not run away from it, do not try to avoid it. It is a gift God gives to us, something special if we receive it in God's love.

— *Fear versus faith*

Fear is rampant in the Church today, but fear is only a sign of a weak faith. There is nothing to be afraid of if you live your life in Christ, Our Lord's, hands, He protects you, He keeps you safe. Today, so many are afraid of an antichrist, of the end times. How foolish that is! If you live in Christ, Our Lord, you will be afraid of nothing because you would know that His victory resides in you. When you give your life to Christ, He places you in the palm of His hand, He looks after you, He protects you, He takes care of you and He brings everything you need into your life. Yes, you may struggle at times, but Jesus gives you joys in those struggles, He gives you strength to carry any cross, He takes the misery from your life and brings happiness into it.

When the Lord was helping me to overcome my fear of death, He showed me heaven and how that is what awaits after death if you trust in Jesus. God offers everyone a happy life and eternal bliss in the life to come. Life is about living in God's love on earth so that you can live eternally in His divine, blissful, glorious love. It is there for all of you.

Our Blessed Mother once said to me, "So many people are fearful in life because they do not accept God's love within completely. They put these little barriers up where they cannot quite trust in Him and so let these little doubts come in. Then things are happening in their lives which maybe are not so good, and at times they even blame God for these."

The problem is that we are looking with worldly eyes, we attach so much importance to this life. We think of the here and now. Yes, this earthly life is important, it is where we can grow in grace to love God more and more. It is a wonderful moment where we can grow in grace, come closer to God, where we can become holier and holier. However, it is not everything. We have to remember the life to come, the eternal life, the glorious life with God. We should be looking beyond this life to eternal life, to Christ, Our Lord. When you start to look to that, when you start to want that, ache for that, when you want to live eternally with Him, then there is no fear anymore. Now you realise what this life really is – it is just a moment and you are no longer afraid of losing it. You come to understand that you will only lose it when God wants you to – not a second sooner. Death is a wonderful blessing, but sadly many people are blind to that, many people are afraid of that, and sadly, in that fear, they are led to do things that they should not do.

— *Trials and suffering*

It is when you love God completely, when you trust in God completely and you accept Him within without conditions, your life becomes complete. You come to see the cares and the worries of life as nothing and you see the things happening in your life not as trials and tribulations but as steps closer to God.

You see them as graces that God offers you to come closer to Him by offering them back to Him. By offering the suffering you have in your life, the troubles you have in your life, offering them to Jesus on the cross to come closer to Jesus, offering them to Him to help other people. Saying, "I accept my sufferings and I accept my problems. Please, Lord, use them in some way to help others come closer to You." Then you will find you come closer to God and you will find your life becomes more complete. You will find the fears, the worries just fall away. You will find the evil one cannot do anything to you. Because once you submit totally to God's love, once you give yourself totally to God, there is nothing evil can do to you unless God wills it and when God wills it, you want to accept it.

The Lord showed me that the evil one can do nothing to you if you give yourself completely to God but so often people do not do that. If we have a little thing happen in our life, something that causes problems, so often we are ready to blame God and to turn away from God or not to trust in Him so much. When people do that, the evil one works inside you to make that little thing larger and larger so that your soul can be taken away just a bit more and a bit more and a bit more. Then you are so far away from God that you do not trust in Him at all and the love seems to disappear. This is how the evil one works because he wants to take you away from God. He works by trying to put fears into you, trying to put doubts into you to take that trust, that love of God away. In these times where you are feeling that way, instead of turning from God, you should be turning to Him. Love Him more. Receive the sacraments more. Pray more. I have found, if you do that, it is a struggle, it really is, but when you do that, you can overcome the evil in your life because God fills you with the graces, with the gifts that you need to overcome it. However, it is up to you to turn to God and ask for these graces, ask for those gifts by submitting totally to His will and saying, "Whatever You want in my life, Lord, I accept."

So often, we find it hard to do this because we have a pride within us that says, "We want to do what we want in our life." Then the moment something goes wrong, "Well, why is God doing this to me? Why is this happening to me and not to someone else?" We feel self-pity, this selfishness within that we all have and we allow it to grow at times. If we can look at that and see what it truthfully is, it is a weakness within us that we all have, and if we can turn to God and ask Him to help us overcome all these weaknesses, He will. Doing so we will find that these weaknesses become strengths. These weaknesses become graces to bring us closer and closer to God to grow in His love.

As we grow in His love, then we can take it to others. It is so important that you do not let fears and frustrations come into your life to take you away from God. In the love of the Father, and Jesus, and the Holy Spirit, you should not be afraid of anything. You should not be worried about anything and you should not care too much about the difficulties that happen in your life because you should know that God is going to look after you because He has promised you He will.

I still have problems happen in my family and happen in my life. Satan does not give up he attacks in so many ways. My son was in intensive care once and he was close to death. I was in England at that time and he was in Australia. The evil one said to me, if I give him my soul he will let my son live. Now I love my son and would give my life for him but I said to satan, "You cannot have my soul, it is Jesus'. You can take my life, if you want, but you cannot take my soul and if my son is to die, that is God's will." When I said that, my son came out of the coma he was in and he was healed and I thank God for that. Once again God showed me what trust in Him brings. At that time I could have been saying, "Well, okay, I want my son to live and I will do that." But I didn't, I trusted in God and He saved my son and helped me to grow closer to Him. I saw trusting in God was the most important thing no matter what pressure the other one puts upon you, no matter what the worries are, how heavy they are, and believe me, that was one of the heaviest things in my life to know my son was dying. It is important to remember in these times if you can offer your struggles to God and trust in God, then you will come closer to Him and God is going to look after you no matter what.

Yet so many of us cannot believe that, can we? At times we feel so frustrated, angry with God at times. We should not feel that way. Understand where that comes from. It comes from the evil one working on you to take you away from God. See what these things in your life truly are and come closer to God by stepping over them in His love and in His mercy.

The ways of the world

When heaven first came to me by the help of heaven and the grace of God I decided to change. This was not something I did easily or willingly in the beginning. I was given a good shake by heaven to help me change my life. Even though when the angel first came who had told me that God loved me and that God wanted my love and that God loved every person, no matter how bad they were, that even the worst sinner in the world was loved by God. Even when the angel told me that, I could not accept God's love into my life.

I had no interest in it. It was only later when the saints came and encouraged me to look back at my life, and to see how I had been living and what it had cost, all the pain that it had brought into my life and into the lives of others. When I looked back at my life by the grace of

God, I started to see things that I had never seen before. First of all, it seemed as if I had been sinning every moment and I saw how I had been totally self-centred, focused on myself, focused on the ways of the world and trying to get everything from the world.

— *The emptiness of the world*
As I looked back, I saw that always within me, no matter what I had from the world, that always there was an emptiness, an insecurity, feelings of being unloved, unwanted, uncared for and so much anger and jealousy. I had little love in my heart, instead I had hatred and bitterness for most people. Looking back, I realised how I was rejecting God and the love He had created me in and the love He had created me to live in. I was shown we are all created to live in God's love and that whether we understand it or not, we exist in His love in every moment. That He has created everything in His love and everything continues to exist in His love. I was shown the moment you stop loving, that you step out of the way that you were created to live and no longer do you live at ease in your life. As I looked back at my life I saw that was so true.

I saw how evil came into my life through sin, through the selfishness and the greed I had. I saw how the evil one had massaged my bad feelings, how he had encouraged my bad thoughts to grow and grow into actions. How, as this happened, he filled me with turmoil and how he made the feelings of being unloved, unwanted, grow and grow. Looking back I saw that the things of addiction, while they may smother these bad feelings for a time, when the effects wore off, these feelings were still there and much stronger which, of course, led me to take more things of addiction. Always I felt there was something missing in my life. I truly was never at peace, never at ease and never happy. Even though I had lots of money and had lots of things of the world, it never was enough. Always I wanted more and more and because of that I hurt so many people in seeking things for myself.

I saw how through my sins, I had opened myself up to evil. I saw how evil had come into my life, how from an early age he had led me to do things I should not have done. From the first time I sinned, even with the least wrong I did, I had invited evil into my life, and every time I sinned, I continued to do so. Every time I sinned I opened my heart, my soul to him. With the smallest sin, a bad thought, a bad word about others, even those turned me away from God and opened me to the evil one.

I saw the fruits of that and I realised that when evil came into my life, all he brought was pain, hurt, suffering, turmoil for me and for others whom I came in contact with. All the evil one wants to do is to hurt us, hurt us eternally, and through my weaknesses and through my sins, evil reached out through me to hurt others. I saw clearly how much pain I had caused others through the bad things that I did and I also saw that living the way I was had caused me so much pain. By my seeking more of the world, thinking only about myself, I had become an unknowing servant of evil.

Evil also encourages the selfishness and the greed to grow. Because the more selfish, the more greedy a person becomes, the more focused they are on the ways of the world instead of the ways of heaven. Then they turn away from God, as in that turning into self, a person closes themselves to God because the more we think of the world, the less we think of heaven. Also when we live the way of the world, we become prisoners of the world, prisoners of evil. Now I looked and realised why I suffered so much in life and why I had hurt others so much and I thought how stupid I had been to live the way of the world. The world gives you so little but it takes so much from you. Constant taxes, constant bills to pay, so many people are depressed or unhappy because their life is full of worries as they struggle to live in this world according to the ways of the world. As they struggle, many of the young turn to drugs and to alcohol, trying to find a little bit of pleasure. Of course they do not realise the price they have to pay for it in this life and in the life to come.

I saw that God had created us in love to live in what He had created in love – the world, the planet. We were meant to exist in love and the moment we stop loving by sinning, we stop living as we should. We step outside of the love of God and we open ourselves to evil and so we have this uneasiness within and life becomes a burden. I began to understand the reason why I had always felt so empty within. My soul was empty of the love of God and nothing could fill my soul with what it needed. Through my sins I was starving my soul. My soul was hungering for God's love and that was the emptiness I was feeling.

The realization came of how foolish I had been. I saw as I embraced the ways of the world, the ways that lead people to greed, to selfishness, to sin, I had turned away from Jesus and accepted the embrace of the evil one even though I did not know it. I realised that the evil one only wants to hurt people. While he may give you some false excitement for a short while, there is always a price to pay. The price is pain, hurt, suffering and misery and unless you repent eventually that price is your eternal soul.

It became clear as I looked back, truly, my life had been miserable. I had never had much peace in my life and I saw that was because of my foolish pride. I also saw that every moment, Jesus had been there, reaching out, offering me an embrace of love. How, if only I had accepted His embrace, He would have brought peace, joy, love and happiness into my life. I saw now so clearly that yes, I may have continued to suffer a little in life, but I saw that Jesus would have been there every moment, easing my suffering, helping carry my crosses for me and bringing a joy and a peace into my life.

Heaven said to me it is not too late, it is never too late to embrace Jesus and to have the joy of His love brought into your life. All Jesus brings into your life is goodness. All Jesus wants is the best for everyone while the evil one only wants the worst for everyone. The saints said, "If you turn to God now, trying to live His way, trying to walk the way of Jesus, then the evil in your life will be overcome."

— *A turning point – turn to God*
I thought, "Life has been so bad, surely there must be something better than that, I will give it a try. Life cannot be just about the things of the world because they are so empty. There must be much more."

When heaven came to me and I was shown how miserable my life truly was, I was shown it did not need to be that way. How, if I accepted the love of God, if I accepted Jesus into my life, life could be happy. At first I thought Jesus would not want someone like me but heaven explained that God wants everyone, He loves everyone. So with the encouragement of heaven I turned to embrace Jesus. I tried to change. Jesus said He forgave me and it was like a weight being lifted from me. I had never felt such love in my life and I will never forget that tender embrace that He gave me. Since that embrace I have never known such happiness, such peace, such contentment. My life has changed completely. All my addictions fell away immediately, in one moment. One day I was an alcoholic, the next day I was not and all because of the love of God. The emptiness I had was taken away and a miserable life became a happy one. I discovered when you embrace Jesus, you find love, joy, happiness – the complete opposite of evil.

This can be the same for everyone if you open your heart and totally embrace Christ. For many people that means a complete change of life. Many are afraid to make that change but they should not be because it is a change for the better.

What this change means is that you have to stop loving yourself first. We have got things the wrong way round. We love ourselves first usually, but we are meant to love God first and foremost, above all others, above all else, above even your self. There is meant to be a burning desire to love God and please God. When you have that desire in your heart and in your very soul, then it is natural that you desire to love others and to put them before yourself. Our life is meant to be a life in imitation of Christ. Where we put God first, we put others before ourselves and we put ourselves last. It is when we do this that God puts us first. This is the complete opposite of what the world teaches you but this is doing what God has always taught us. Yet many of us keep rejecting this and we keep suffering.

Since Jesus came into my life in every moment, even the most difficult ones, there has been a deep joy inside me. Ever since, I have never felt lonely again. I still have crosses to carry, I still have difficulties, but always I feel happy inside because I know Jesus is with me and no matter what the situation, He will bring the best from it. He always does. He has never let me down.

— *Trapped by self*
As I travel the world, I meet many Christians, many Catholics and many are leading miserable lives, feeling lonely, unloved, uncared for. They cannot even love themselves properly. What a shame it is that

we have been blinded so much. Evil leads us into self and into the world and away from God because evil wants to hurt us and through our selfishness and our sins, it can so easily.

As I look at the people I meet, I see that so many have the same bad feelings inside that I had, feelings of being so lonely, so much jealousy, depression. These are the things that sin brings into lives by tempting us to look at self and away from God. Every time we think of self first, we are denying Christ. Every time we are seeking more and more for self, feeling so greedy, we deny Christ and we turn away from Christ. Yet still we think we are Christian.

Often so many Catholics who come to church think they have a full life in Christ and do not realise that they only have a partial life in Christ because they are not living every moment for Him and are not living to His way.

When heaven encouraged me to change, I was told that I was living the wrong way round, that I was putting myself first in all things and that I should be putting God first in all things. I should be putting others before myself and always putting myself last. I found that was very difficult for me in the beginning to understand and to accept because I was so used to putting myself first. Frequently it seems Christians do the same, they put themselves first. Then they may consider their family and friends, but so often they make excuses to ignore the poor and the needy in the world and God comes way down the list and when they do come to God in prayer so often they are just demanding from God.

So many of those who even think they are devout – because they come to Mass frequently, they may come to prayer groups – but many of these same people, when they leave the church and go out into the world, they are just like everyone else and blend in with others. They accept all the ways of the world and they seem to forget about Christ. For many people, God is in the church, in the prayer groups, among their family or friends, but in the wide world, God is pushed aside and they forget about Him. They replace God with other things because now money becomes more important than God. Pleasure, excitement and things of the world come before God. How the evil one laughs because so easily he can bring people's focus on the world and away from heaven. He gets them to focus on themselves and their needs, on their desires, and all of a sudden, life becomes self-centred and not God-centred as the world draws you into self-centredness, seeking more money, more things of the world, more excitement, more pleasure. It is in that self-centredness you are being led into more and more sins. It usually starts with a small little sin, but then you do bigger and bigger sins, and all of a sudden you are so far away from God, you wonder how you got there.

Around the world I meet Catholics who are living a little bit as I did, many who have accepted little sins in their life and then through these little sins, let evil in to lead them to do or to accept bigger and bigger sins. Often they have come to sin without even thinking about it. They forget every time you sin, every time you accept a wrong of the world, you turn away from Jesus, deny Jesus and invite evil into your life. Every time you turn away from someone in need, you turn away from Jesus and embrace the evil one. Every time you gossip about someone, you turn away from Christ and embrace evil. Every time in your pride you condemn and judge others, you are turning away from Christ and embracing evil. Today so many Catholics are like other people who, maybe unknowingly, invite the evil one into their lives with their acceptance of things like homosexuality, divorce, abortion, contraception and much more.

As we invite the evil one into our lives, while he may give us some little excitement for a moment, always he demands a high price. As you look back at the history of the world, you can see the price he has demanded and that has been paid. The history of the world is full of pain, of hurt, of suffering, and truly no peace. Yet in our foolishness, we keep turning to the ways of the world, we perpetuate the misery and the suffering but it does not need to be like that. Unfortunately people today, as I did, keep embracing the world before Christ. They think that in the things of the world they would find the answers to life and then people wonder why their lives are so unhappy. However, it should be obvious to everyone that when you put self and the world before God, you invite unhappiness into your life. You invite turmoil and suffering into your life because when you become self-centred, you sin. When you put self and the world first, you reject God. Even though you may come to Mass on Sundays or even every day, if your life is self-centred and not God-centred, you close your heart to God.

By putting yourself first in all things and ignoring God and ignoring others, you sin. You are led into lying, into bad thoughts, into jealousy, into so many bad things, and you are led to accept the wrongs of the world and you forget the rights of God.

In our life today, the world is such a disaster, so much suffering, and the reason is that the majority of people think about self instead of thinking of God. If we are thinking of God, then we will be happy and we will all be sharing and caring for each other, we would all have good standards of living and good health care. Everyone would be happy and there would be no wars, no killing, no sin, but satan is there to build up our self with so-called good messages about our rights today which really are our wrongs. So many people seek wealth, position, fame but they still have loneliness in their heart, insecurity, wondering if people really love them, what is life all about and that is because in all those worldly things and so called rights there is little unless you know the love of God. When you know the love of God, if you have these things of the world, you will want to use them to help other people. Because you see that God has created others and that God loves them as He loves you, and in that case, you should love them and you should help them as well. You realise it is the right of others to have a good life too.

— *Sin is a cancer*
Sin is a cancer of the soul. When you let that cancer in as small sin, unless you stop that and turn to God through confession and changing your life, then you are drawn into bigger and bigger sins and that cancer eats away your soul. It envelopes your soul to close your heart and soul to God and the more it does, the more it fills your life with darkness because of the evil that surrounds you. This is why so many people are unhappy, so many people are depressed. As when your soul is in this state, it cries out in agony because it is created to exist in God's love and for God's love and it longs to return into God's love. So now as your soul is aching inside you, that affects your mind, your body, your being, and life becomes so unhappy.

61

This is what the way of self and the way of the world brings you. It never brings true happiness and you only have to look around the world to see that. I have been in the medical industry and one of the biggest drug types are the anti-depressives. In the western world, people have so much and yet there is so much depression. So many people see psychologists, psychiatrists. So many people are not happy, so many miserable people.

We put the world and self first, and then maybe our family, and then maybe God. When we live our life this way, we are actually turning away from God and inviting hurt into our lives. When you put God first in your life, before all else, before even yourself, then God brings goodness into your life, more than you could ever desire, He is there with you, looking after you, taking care of you. Today, many people foolishly are blind to this. No wonder our lives are so confused.

Looking back at my life, I saw that when I first started to sin, I had some guilt about what I did but as time went on, there was no guilt because evil had eaten away at my conscience and destroyed it. God gives us a conscience so that we know what is right and wrong. I had allowed the world and sin to destroy my conscience and as time went on, I had no guilt at all and I would do any sin. It started with my committing small sins then evil led me to bigger ones. In the end I was committing sins which years before, I would never have imagined I could have done. Now I saw how foolish I had been, for as I looked back, I saw how unhappy my life had been. Even though I had many things of the world, I never was truly happy and always there was an emptiness inside.

— *Grey areas*

So many Catholics do not realise that the world brings you to focus on self and not on God. That is where evil wants your focus – on self because when you are looking to self, you can be easily drawn into sin. Evil can easily get you to accept sin or to remain silent in the face of sin, to find nothing wrong with things that God rejects. How satan laughs when so many Catholics accept things like divorce, contraception or abortion and just blend in with the rest of the world. Many sit back quietly and do not oppose these evils. It is when you do not stand against these things, you accept them into your life and you are opening yourself to the evil one. Others, while they may oppose some of the more obvious things like homosexuality, still keep quiet about the waste in the world and those who are starving, those who are in need. So many do not help the poor, as they should, because they are too busy helping themselves. Many of us are quiet about the wrongs in the world and accept them or do nothing to stop them growing. By this passivity, you accept sin, you become part of sin. I used to do that and I used to make many excuses for sin but there are no excuses for sin that are acceptable.

When you pray and you keep your focus on God, He will reach out to you and by the power of His Holy Spirit lift you up to higher levels of grace. When this began to happen to me, it was like scales fell from my eyes. Now things looked so different. As I looked to the world and looked to my life, everything now was black or white, it was either right or it was wrong, there was no in between, no grey areas.

You are either with God or you are not. The Lord showed me that these grey areas are actually areas of the dark and as a Christian you must make every attempt to live in the light at all times. You must try and love at all times. So many of us try to have a foot in each camp, we make excuses for sin and we still think we are holding on to Jesus and living His way.

Before, I never really recognised sin and all the bad things, many of them, I just accepted as the way of life. The commandments and the teachings of the Catholic Church I took little notice of and I took more notice of the ways of the world. Now I saw how wrong that had been because I saw that the Church teachings and the commandments of God were there to lead you to a good, a happy life and that if I was obedient to them at all times, I would be protected from all evil.

This is because God, through His commandments and His Holy Catholic Church pours out so powerfully the grace of His Holy Spirit to guide you along the right path, the path to heaven. It became clear that the Church and the commandments of God are like a cocoon of love to protect you from evil. So many people have forgotten this and I was one of them. I used to have these grey areas and I'd say, "Well, I like this commandment, I will obey that one, but I do not like this one, I'll ignore it." Today many people have these grey areas where they hide their sin or their acceptance of sin. They choose which commandments they will obey and cover the guilt they feel inside for doing so with foolish reasons.

When you look to the world, you are drawn into the world and you are seduced by the world, seduced by evil to accept all the wrong things, making excuses for them and still think you are living the way of Jesus. What a blind pride it is, that so many of us have. We live the way of the world and in living that way, we are turning away from Jesus, we are denying Jesus. As we are turning away from Him, we turn towards the evil one who waits for us with his arms open wide to embrace us with suffering, with pain, with hurt.

In our lives, we are meant to look beyond the world, to look to heaven in all we do and to focus on the eternal life to come. So that we can come to that never-ending life in heaven – but to reach that life in heaven, we have to look to where we want to go. We have to look to heaven in all we do.

— *What the world offers you*
Life is a joyful gift from God that He gives to every person but you can only find the fullness of joy, of peace and happiness in every moment by living for God, with God and in God. For about fifteen years now, I have just worked for God and have done nothing else and every moment has been one of happiness. He said to me, "If you give your life to me, I will give you all you need." He does and He will do the same for everyone else because He loves you all the same as He loves me. All He asks is that we let go of the things of the world and hold on to Him.

A large number of people wonder why they are unhappy. When I talk to some of them it is so obvious it is because most of their life is focused on the world and not on God. No wonder they are miserable. That is what the things of the world bring you. When you love money, there is never enough. You have always got to have more and more and you do not want to part from it, you do not want it to leave you. Often you try to spend as little as possible, trying to get other people to pay for things you should pay for. What a miserable life that is. When you are with such people, you do not want to be with them. The unhappiness in their life touches your life. Evil is infectious. When it touches one life and makes it unhappy, it reaches out through that life to make others unhappy.

Some Catholics try to have their heaven on earth by having all the things of the world. People work long hours to get more and more money to get maybe a new car or have another holiday but these are just temporary things that do not bring you true happiness. Some, because they are focused on the world, are miserable. My prayer is that they will discover what I did – that this is the wrong way to live. The things of the world are just temporary. The things of God are eternal.

If you look at the billionaires, the rock stars, the movie stars, they have everything. However, so many of them cannot have true relationships and divorce and marry many times. So many of them are addicted to drugs or to other things. Many are unhappy and depressed. Many have to see a psychiatrist. Many commit suicide. They have got everything of the world and they are so miserable. This is what the world gives you. Yet so many people look up to them and want what they have. How blind we are, how foolish we are!

Life is a joyful gift that God gives to every person and if you live in the way that God asks – He does not demand, he asks gently in love because He loves you – if you live the way He asks, the good way, a happy life can be yours. It can be anyone's. It is when you live for Him, God brings your life to fullness in the world and gives you all you need.

Now is the time to change. If every Catholic would live their faith as they are meant to, hold on firmly to the truth of Christ, deny the world and put Christ first in all things, then life would be so different. It is when you put Christ first that He brings into your life all you need. He never leaves you alone. He takes away all the bad feelings of being unloved, unwanted, of being less than others. He gives you the strength to endure anything joyfully in Him. No longer does life become a burden. Each moment becomes joyful as you celebrate in each moment Christ's love for you.

As you live in this way, God changes your life, and through you He changes the lives of those around you as you become true vessels of grace as you are meant to be. It is when a billion Catholics start to live their faith in the way they are meant to, the grace of God will pour out so powerfully, that the light of Christ will illuminate the world through these Catholics to disperse the dark and bring paradise to earth. But remember it begins with each one of you.

From the beginning I was told that God is love and that God had created everything in love. The universe, the world, us, the very air we breathe. Everything is created in God's love and we are created to exist in God's love and so to exist properly in His love, we have to love. The moment you stop loving, you allow evil into your life.

The meaning of life is to love, love God and love each other. It is very simple but we try to complicate things. If only we could live as God asks then all sin, all evil would be overcome in our lives because pure love is more powerful than the strongest evil. Pure love is found in your Catholic faith, in Jesus Christ, Our Lord.

— *The vision of the fish*
I was given a vision once by Jesus. He showed me a fish swimming in water and He said, "Look, the fish is happy, it has everything in life." Then the fish was taken out of the water and placed on the bank. The fish gasped and struggled and was dying until it was placed back into the water where it came to full life again and was comfortable in the water surrounding it.

Jesus said, "Mankind is like this. When it lives outside of My love, it is like the fish on the bank, gasping and struggling to live but when mankind lives in My love, it lives a full life just as the fish does in the water."

— *Struggling to love others*

Many Catholics today find it hard to love. We can love maybe our husband, our wife, our children, our close family but so often it is hard to love others and often we are even drawn to hatred towards others. That is not the life God has called us to. God has called us to love everyone, to see everyone as a brother or a sister. To love even those who would hurt you, those who would kill you. That is what Christ did and as Christians, as imitators of Christ, we are meant to do the same. Some Catholics today, if someone says a bad word about them, they find it so hard to forgive and often feel resentment inside. Someone hurt you so you want revenge. So often, we are drawn into hatred and still we call ourselves Catholic. No Catholic should have an air of hatred within them because the moment they do, then they are not living the way of Christ.

To find the power and the strength to love as Jesus calls us to, we have to turn to Him and ask Him for that strength because in ourselves, in our humanity, we can struggle to love. It is so easy to get frustrated, to get angry with people who do not listen to you, who do not want to do what you want them to do. It is easy to feel bitter and to seek revenge.

However, that is not the way of Christ. The way of Christ is to love and to love and to love and to forgive everyone anything. How many Catholics truly do that? How many can truly say they live that way, the way of love which is Christ's way? We are meant to be vessels of love, that is what God calls us to and to be those vessels, to have the strength to love, we have to come to Jesus in the Eucharist and lean on Him. We have to turn to Him and say, "Help me, Lord, I cannot do it but You help me, You show me how to love."

The way of Christ is the way of forgiving love. I know tonight there are some people here who find it hard to talk to some of their family members. Well, if you cannot love and forgive your close family, how can you love anyone else? We are called to look beyond these worldly ways because that is what they are. We are called to look to heaven and the ways of heaven, which are love and forgiveness for all people. If you show forgiving love at all times, then you show Christ. If not, then you only show yourself and you allow the evil one to work through yourself to hurt you and to hurt others.

When I was asked to change and live the way of love, I found it very difficult because I am not a man who loves easily, believe me. I was a man full of hatred and now God was calling me to love God above all, above all others, above even myself, and to love fellow man, to love everyone. To place others before myself and I really struggled with that for a long time. At times, I still do. I travel a lot, I get tired, I get irritable and sometimes it is very hard to show love.

Saint Teresa of Avila once said to me, "You are trying to overcome your weaknesses yourself. That is impossible. You need God to help you overcome them." She said to remember this saying, "In me my weakness, in God my strength." It is true because this helps me to realise how truly weak I am. However, I understand now that it does not matter how weak I am, that if I give myself totally to God, He will give me the strength of His love to live the right way and to enjoy living life as I am meant to.

So every day I ask the Holy Spirit to help me to overcome my weaknesses and to live in love. The moment I open my eyes, I ask the Holy Spirit to give me the grace to live every moment for God and to give myself in every moment to God and to focus totally on God. Now the most wonderful thing is that the Holy Spirit is always there! When I fall down He reaches out to lift me up. When I feel I cannot love He shows me Jesus suffering on the cross. Showing me no matter how much Jesus suffered, no matter how much Jesus hurt, no matter how much pain He endured, still He loved. Reminding me if I want to truly be Catholic then I must love in my weakness too. I saw that in my self it is impossible to do this because I am so full of pride but that with the help of the Holy Spirit it is possible.

What the Holy Spirit does, every time I have a bad thought coming into my mind, He reminds me to love. Every time I say stupid words, and I seem to do that every day, He reminds me that is not the way Christ speaks and neither should I. He shows me the moment I turn away from anyone, reject anyone, I am rejecting Christ. The moment I deny anyone my love, I am denying Christ. The moment I think of anyone as less than me, I am denying Christ. I saw that as Christ opened His Heart to all, so every Christian is meant to open their hearts to all. Now every time I struggle in loving, I turn to the

Holy Spirit and then He shows me, in everyone I have turned away from, the face of Jesus and He reminds me in doing so I have turned away from Jesus. Then I have to turn back to that person and show them love. How can I not as there is Jesus before me! Sadly today, so many Christians, so many Catholics do not live their faith that way, as for many Catholics love does not come into their faith but love must be the centre of your faith because God is love.

As I began to ask the Holy Spirit to help me show love at all times, when I had a bad thought about someone, the Holy Spirit would show me Jesus on the cross, suffering and dying. He shows me Jesus did this for everyone because He loves all and soon those bad thoughts would leave. Any time someone hurt me, again, I saw Jesus suffering and dying and I realised that He was hurt for love, so I too must accept that hurt and respond in love. Every time it becomes so difficult to love because there are so many crosses, so many struggles, every time there is the Holy Spirit, guiding me back to Jesus showing me His love so that in His love, I can have the strength to carry on loving. In myself I realised I can do nothing, I am so weak but in God, all good is possible and all evil can be overcome if only you accept God completely into your life and allow His love to strengthen you.

The Lord, Jesus, once said to me, "Every time you find it hard to love, look to Me on the cross. See that no matter how much you hurt Me, I suffered for you, I died for you because I love you. See that I love everyone else exactly the same. If you want to truly love Me, then you must love others as I love them, no matter how much they hurt you, no matter how much they abuse you. Yes, even if they kill you, open your arms, your heart, in love of them. Knowing as you do so, My divine love pours out through you, united with your love, to change the world."

He explained this is the faith the early Church understood with so many people who were willing to give their lives joyfully for the love of God and the love of others. This is why we have this Church today. Yet, so many of us have forgotten that love, we are blind to how we are living. Blind to how are we giving our children their Church in the future. Are we giving them a Church full of the love of

Christ or a Church full of love of self? I wonder what the early martyrs think as they look down from heaven and see how we live and how we love?

Heaven also showed me that the Catholic, Eucharistic faith that the Lord gave us is the faith of love. I saw also the reason why so many people struggle with their faith. They have forgotten love. Many people just go through the routine of faith, doing their duty, saying their prayers with no love in them. Doing this we are no different than the Sadducees and Pharisees of Jesus' time. When Jesus came, He said we have to be different, we have to love. Love at all times, in all ways, all people. Love unto death but how many Catholics live this way today? So many Catholics have anger, hatred, bitterness, resentment. When you have these things in your heart you do not have love in your heart. When you live a self-centred life, you do not have love in your heart.

We have never been called to live alone. We have always been called to live with God in a partnership of love. However, most Catholics have forgotten that, and so often try to live their faith in themselves and not in God.

Catholicism is the faith of love. Without love, our faith is empty and for many Catholics, that is why their life is empty. It is empty because they are living in the world instead of living in the love of Christ. In His Eucharistic love, He brings your life in the world to fullness because when you leave the church with Christ inside you, you are full of Christ and every step you are taking, Jesus is taking with you.

Every time you are reaching out to someone, Christ is reaching out with you. Every time you are trying to love someone, Christ is loving with you. Every cross you have to carry He carries with you and gives you the strength to carry. This is the life we are meant to live; every moment with Christ, in Christ and through Christ. It is only when you live that way, you can truly know the fullness of life, the fullness of God's love and the fullness of peace.

This is the faith Christ, Our Lord, gave to us but so many of us Catholics, because we are blinded by pride and self, we push it aside and embrace the world. How foolish we are!

71

— The example of Jesus

Our Blessed Mother told me once, "You are never meant to live your faith by yourself. Do not try and show love by yourself. If you try to love in yourself and by yourself, you are bound to fail because satan will work on you, work on your pride, to stop you loving or to change your love to that which is not true love. Remember he is very powerful, he is a fallen archangel, he is stronger than you. However, if you turn to the Holy Spirit and ask the Holy Spirit to help you live every moment in love and persevere in the asking, then you will find as time goes on the Holy Spirit strengthens you with His grace. He gives you the strength to open your heart in love to all. God has called you to a partnership with Him and if you try to play your part, if you try to love as Christ loved, then God will give you all the grace you need but you must first ask Him for it."

Without love in life, life is empty and without a full love in your life, you cannot know true life. It is the same in your relationship with others. When you reach out to others in love, you are doing as you are supposed to and Jesus reaches out with you in love. So here is God and man, united in love, reaching out to help someone else with a full love. Every time I find it hard to love, the Holy Spirit reminds me that I cannot love fully by myself, I need God to help me love and so the Holy Spirit reminds me to keep asking Jesus to help me to love. It is when you keep asking that over and over, no longer do you have any hatred upon your heart. No longer do you have any bitterness, any resentment or jealousy. You even want to love those who hurt you. You even want to love those who are deep in sin because you know this is the way that Christ loved. You also see now through eyes of love that those who sin, those who want to hurt you, they have a weakness in their heart, in their soul that the evil one reaches into to manipulate them to do these bad things.

When you see that, no longer can you feel angry or bitter towards anyone because now you feel sorry for them as you see how the evil one is using them and then you can only respond in love and in prayer for them. Then you end up with a passionate love of Christ because now you see how in His passion, those who abused Him, those who hurt Him, those who killed Him, He did not condemn them, He did not judge them. You see how He reached out in love to them, in forgiveness as He saw how the evil one was manipulating these people. That is how it must be for us. We must never hate anyone, we must never feel bad about anyone, bitter about anyone or resent anyone because the moment we do, we open ourselves to the evil one who only wants to come into our life and hurt us and draw us into eternal suffering. Foolishly today, many Catholics allow this to happen, influenced by the world to stop loving and to be selfish.

When I asked the saints, "How can I love at all times? It seems so hard," they explained that Jesus, God Himself, came to earth to show us how we can love in Him. That by walking the way of Christ, we can devote our lives to God and offer our whole lives in love to God the Father and the Son and the Holy Spirit. Walking the way of Christ is walking the way of love, living every moment for God. Not just living for Him in the church but when you go out to the world, putting Him first in all things.

Many of the saints said to me, "It will be difficult, it will not be easy, but if you look to our lives, you will see that by the grace of God and by the power of the Holy Spirit we overcame our weaknesses to walk the way of Christ. In His life, Christ showed to love God the Father first and foremost in all things and to love each other and to forgive each other even unto death. If you want to live the way God created you to, live the way He showed you. As you live that way, you remain in His love and you become full of His peace, His happiness and His security."

They explained it is no wonder there is so much suffering in the world today because people have not learnt from history. God gave the Jewish people the commandments and they kept ignoring them and they suffered. Then Jesus came to earth and He showed us how to live and we continue to ignore Him and we suffer. They said, "If you want to have peace in your life and peace in your world, you must live the way of Christ, obedient to the commandments." So I tried to do that and as I did, I was so surprised because now in every moment, I was feeling love and contentment within me. My hatred for other people just disappeared to be replaced by love for everyone.

— *The example of the apostles*

The apostles explained to me that when Christ came to earth, He called them to be different. He called all the disciples to be different, not the same as everyone else in the world. That all the saints lived their life in that way, being different to others, living their life for God, in that way showing love of God and growing in love of God. That call is exactly the same for each one of you today, each one of you is called to be different, not the same as everyone else. By our baptism, by our faith, we have been set aside to be different to everyone else.

Just as He did with the apostles, God sets us aside to be the lights in the dark so that as people look at us, they can see the light of Christ in us, and in the light of Christ, find the true way to live. We are not meant to accept the ways of the world but gently and lovingly live the ways of Christ. Not condemning and judging others, instead always reaching out with a loving hand to guide everyone we meet to Christ Our Lord. Using our lives as examples by never accepting any sin, any wrong, no matter how small it is.

We should be the apostles of today through whom Christ can change the world for the better. We are meant to be lights in the dark, standing lovingly but firmly against all that is wrong and if we do not do it, how are people to see the light of Christ?

Many Catholics and many Christians find this hard because they think if they are different from the rest of the world, people would see them as crazy, as religious nuts, and so it is much easier to accept what everybody else accepts. That is not how you are meant to live. The truth is that when you do not live the way of Christ, you are truly crazy. Now is the time to break this circle of stupidity and in true wisdom accept the ways of God into our lives.

By your baptism, by being Christian and by living the fullness of Christianity which is Catholicism, each one of you is meant to be different from the others in the world. You are meant not to accept what is wrong in the world but to oppose it. Not just to blend in with everyone else, but to stand out and be lights in the dark by gently proclaiming the loving truth of Christ, Our Lord, and never being afraid to do so. Not doing it in condemnation and judgement of others, but in love of others as that is Christ's way.

This is what the early Church did, unafraid they stood up, they were different. By them living the way of Christ, they gave us the Church we have today. I wonder what sort of Church we are giving our children and our grandchildren? Most of us just blend in with everyone else accepting and taking part in the wrongs of the world, not standing against them as we are supposed to. When you do that, you are Christian in name only. To be Christian, to be Catholic means to live the way of Christ and proclaim His way to everyone. It is when we live this way that we open our hearts and souls to the grace of God. Grace that He will pour through us to touch the world and change the world.

In these times so many people complain about the state of the world and they blame everyone else. They blame the governments, they blame the Church, the priests – anyone but themselves, forgetting that the world is the way it is because of us. It is because we are so quiet and not living the way of Christ, not living our faith as we are meant to. We have allowed the world and its ways to change us, to change our faith instead of letting Christ in us, through our faith, through us, change the world.

God gives us the opportunity today, where the world is so empty of God and so full of self, He gives us the chance to be examples like the apostles or the early disciples, He gives us the opportunity to be living examples of Christ's love. Unfortunately so many Catholics today complain about the lack of faith in the world, and they either do not see the opportunity or do not want to accept the opportunity that God is giving them to reach out to the world in His love so as to change it. It is when you accept this duty, because truly it is your duty, God guarantees you sainthood in heaven.

— *The Western world and the loss of faith*
So many Catholics in the west are complaining about how Catholicism is slipping away. Instead of complaining, we should thank God for this golden opportunity to be the new apostles, the new disciples of today. Looking back at the early Church, seeing how they, against all opposition, went out and spread the love of God in the world, knowing that if we do the same as they did, that God would pour His grace out in abundance and change this world.

In these times many Catholics try and have it both ways, they live the way of the world and try to blend it into the way of God. Jesus told us we cannot do that, you cannot serve mammon and serve God. You have to make a decision in your life, the decision to be with God or against God. I meet many people who complain to me about the problems they have in their lives, the difficulties and they do not seem to understand that when we do not live the way of Christ, we are inviting the problems upon ourselves. It is when we live away from Christ, we open ourselves to evil and evil brings suffering into our lives by drawing us more and more into self.

When you focus on self and focus on the world, you will be unhappy because you are focusing just where the evil one wants you to focus. When you look to self and to the world, you are looking away from God and you open yourself to evil. Most of you know it is true because many Catholics know that years ago when they first started to do things that were not quite right, they had feelings of uneasiness within. When they started accepting the wrongs of the world within, they knew it was not right. However, the more they accepted these things, the less they had feelings of uneasiness and then they were led to accept bigger and bigger wrongs.

It is no wonder people are unhappy. No wonder people feel so insecure at times and it is hard to find true love and true peace because when people live this way, the way of the world, their soul is crying within them. It is screaming out from all the pain that they have invited within their soul. So you cannot be at peace with yourself. No wonder there are so many depressed people in the world. No wonder so many people look for love in the wrong places. If you lack the peace in yourself and if you do not love yourself, how can you love others? It is obvious that today people embrace the world but they do not embrace it in the right way. They embrace the world before God and are drawn into the ways of the dark, and as they put the world first, they invite crosses upon themselves. It is when we live the way of Christ, we have love, happiness, joy, peace and contentment in us, but foolishly so many of us keep choosing the way of suffering instead of the way of peace.

— Peace versus confusion

When I started to ask the help of the Holy Spirit to make each moment of my life a prayer of love of God, my life truly was changing and inside me I was filled with peace. Not just a fleeting peace that disappeared after a short time, but a peace that was with me in every moment. In that peace came contentment and happiness. As I tried to live the way of Jesus, that emptiness that I had known before disappeared and I wondered why this happened.

Our Blessed Mother and the Holy Spirit later explained that when you walk the way of Jesus every day and try to live it in every moment, then your heart, your very soul is opened to God. Then in every moment His grace is reaching inside of you and filling you bringing into your heart that peace, that joy and that contentment. I noticed that the moment I was not living the way of Jesus I did not feel quite the same inside, the confusion seemed to come back.

In life it is the same for many people, many Catholics. They live their religious life only in the church, maybe they come to Mass and to prayer groups, but when they leave the church, they forget all about Jesus or they think so little about Him at times. When in fact, you should be doing the reverse, you should be thinking of Him always.

Your life as a Christian is meant to be a life like Christ's, an imitation of His life and just as Christ, Our Lord, when He walked the earth looked to heaven in every moment, so are we meant to. By keeping our focus on heaven, we keep ourselves open to God's grace. However, it is when we look away from heaven and look into self and into the world, then we close ourselves to that grace and it is so easy to look away and to be drawn into the temptations of the world and to start living like everyone else does.

The reason that happens so often is because we forget to ask the Holy Spirit to help us keep our focus on heaven. At the times that I start to look away, the Holy Spirit reminds me, "Look to the Father, look to Jesus and live His way." He reminds me that any time I have a bad thought about others, I am not thinking in a Christian way, I am not thinking like Jesus. Any time I gossip about others, I am not being like Jesus, He never did that. Any time I lie, I cheat, I swindle, I am not doing what Jesus did. Any time I have an angry or bitter thought, any time I think of revenge, any time I cannot forgive, I do not follow Christ. Any time I am greedy, any time I look away from people in need I do not live like Christ. Any time I put the things of the world first, I am not doing what Jesus did.

Yet many Catholics do this and then they cannot see they are not walking the way of Christ and they do not realise that they are being drawn away from Christ and into the ways of evil. No wonder people have so much confusion, pain and hurt in their lives because when you turn to the ways of evil, the evil one does not bring any good, he just wants to torment you.

The foolish thing is that so many Catholics wonder why God allows the confusion in their lives. Why does God not make things much clearer? But God has made it clear. The problem is that we are blinded, blinded by self and blinded by the world. Then in our pride, we blame God for the problems that we ourselves invite into our lives. God is love. He created man in His image. We are meant to be an image of love. The moment we stop loving we turn away from God and we turn into the dark, even though we may not understand it.

Sadly, that has been the history of mankind, from when Adam and Eve first sinned, mankind has continuously been turning away from God and turning into the arms of the evil one. Mankind's history is a history of foolishness, suffering and pain and all caused by mankind itself! But in our blind pride, we blame God for it. However, things can change if every person will just turn back to God in every day in every moment.

Well, it is easy to say, isn't it, but maybe hard to do. But what you will find is, yes, you may fall down at times, yes, you may struggle at times, but the Holy Spirit will be there to lift you up, to help you. God knows you will struggle, but all He wants you to do is, do your best. Try your hardest to live the way of Jesus, and if you do that, then you will open more and more to God's grace and as you are opened to that grace, it will bring that peace, that contentment into your life. The confusion, the turmoil, they will all disappear.

Life becomes so clear. When you have this grace in you every moment now it is so hard for evil to get hold of you. It is so hard for the evil one to bring suffering into your life. Also what happens through you is that God pours out grace to touch your family, to touch your friends, to touch all the people around you and to start changing their lives. This is how the world is brought back to God by each one of you deciding to be imitators of Christ, to be Christian, deciding to live every moment every day for Him.

— *The love of God and the love in the family*
When the saints first told me that I must love God first before myself, before my wife, my family, before my country, before anything, I thought that would be impossible to do.

I thought that maybe if I love God before my wife, it would lessen my love for her but the saints told me the reverse was true. So with their encouragement I was trying to love God in everything I did. The more I did it, the easier it became. I saw that it should be natural for me to love God first. That God has created me, my wife, my children, my family, my friends. He has given me all that is good and so it now seemed a natural thing to love God and to want to love Him more.

I found that my life changed as now my love for my wife grew stronger and stronger. My love for my family, for my friends, for everyone seemed to be increasing and increasing. The hatred and anger I used to have towards other people just seemed to fall away. I came to understand that as you try to love God first, He increases your love for everyone else. This seems to be a very hard thing for many people to do because so often they put God after their family, after their money, after their country, after their job, after anything really. God seems to come way down the list in lives instead of being first in lives.

I saw that so clearly in recent times with the Iraqi war. Many people in the USA, in Australia, in England would say, "We have to put our country first, our President first, our Prime Minister first." I would say, "What about God and what He teaches us?" Sometimes they would say, "Oh, that is different, that does not count. You have to put your country first." How foolish that is to put anything before God because the moment you do so, whether it is country, whether it is self, whether it is anything, you step away from God.

As Christians, as Catholics it is our duty to put the Father, and the Son and the Holy Spirit first in all things. Even above the laws of our country. I follow the laws of my country and of any country as long as they agree with God, but the moment they do not, I do not follow them and do not agree with them. This is the way it must be for every Christian if they want to imitate Christ. Imitating Christ means putting God first in all things. Even giving your life if necessary for God and being obedient to His will, not man's will. Sadly today many call themselves Christians and walk the way of the world instead of the way of God.

Sharing God with others

When the Lord Jesus walked the earth, He brought the love of God to every person. He went out to show every person the way to heaven. As imitators of Christ, we are meant to do the same. It seems many Catholics do not do that. Many Christians do not want to speak up for Christ or live the way of Christ, as they may fear being made fun of, being called crazy. So they just live like everyone else and accept the wrongs of the world.

In fear we allow sin to grow in the world and by our inactive faith we allow souls to be taken away from God. We should go out to every person showing them Christ through our lives. If people laugh at us, hurt us or kill us, we are to thank God for that because then we imitate Christ. All this happened to Him and so we should not be surprised if it happens to us. Yet so many Christians complain about the bad in the world and the lack of faith. Then they sit back and do nothing. How can they claim to truly love God? If you really love God, you have to take Him to others, you cannot stop yourself, you cannot help yourself, you have to do it! There is an ache inside you, which is driving you on and on to share His love with others.

— *The importance of baptism*
How many of you know people who are not baptised – and there are many of them – and yet you keep silent and say nothing. We should be

gently and kindly, not forcefully, reaching out and explaining to them how important baptism is.

If people are not baptised, their souls bear the stain of original sin. There is a big doorway on their soul for evil to enter through and evil can reach inside and take hold to bring those who are not baptised to think they do not need God or lead them to not believing in God. All they believe in is the here and now of this world or some new age things. If we would reach out and explain this to those who are not baptised, then the evil which is attacking them through the weakness of original sin on their soul can be stopped. As it is through baptism, this weakness is washed away through Jesus Christ, Our Lord. In the holy sacrament, Jesus draws us into His death and then into new life with Him and also with the anointing of the Holy Spirit, gifts and graces are offered to us.

Unfortunately, so many people lean back and say nothing but if you do not say anything, don't you see that you are allowing a soul to be taken away from God and when you face Jesus, He is going to ask you, "Why did you say nothing?"

What a shame it is that we keep these wonderful treasures of the sacraments for ourselves. We should go out and tell all people how wonderful the sacraments are. If you do that, yes, it is true not everyone will listen, but some will and some will be drawn to Christ through you and find salvation in Him. If this happens, there is a glory waiting for you in heaven because now you are united with God in His work of salvation.

— *Witnessing to Muslims*

Today so many Catholics are afraid to speak of their faith, certainly afraid to speak to Muslims about it. Afraid in case they get hurt or killed and how the evil one laughs because we are so afraid. There should be no fear in our lives. Just as we should speak to everyone about Jesus, we should speak to our Muslim brothers and sisters but if you cannot find the strength to do that, then you should at least be praying for them to embrace Jesus. Every time I go past a mosque, I pray that anyone who goes in there would be converted and brought to Catholicism. Any time I see a Muslim and I cannot speak to them, I pray that they be converted and brought to Catholicism. All Catholics should be doing that but most do not even think about it and most are too afraid to even show Christ to a Muslim.

I have spoken to Muslims many times and I was afraid in the beginning, but God said, "Do not worry to speak to them in love." I found many of them are interested and want to hear. So if you see a Muslim and you have a prayer card with you of Jesus or Our Lady, just give it to them and say, "Here is a gift for you, God bless you." You will find many of them accept it as they know Jesus and love His Blessed Mother and through this one simple act, you may help to convert a soul. Our faith is there to be lived and to be shared and not to be kept to yourself.

— *Speaking to Protestants*
Around the world we have many Protestant brothers and sisters who love Christ, and they live good lives, trying to live to the Word of God, trying to worship God. Sometimes Catholics are afraid to talk to Protestants about our faith. This may be because our Protestant brothers and sisters usually know Holy Scripture backwards, and most Catholics know so little about Holy Scripture. All this shows is that we do not know our faith.

We should be going out to our Protestant brethren and inviting them lovingly into the fullness of Christ in Catholicism. To do that, not only do we need to know our faith but also their faith. When God showed me the history of the Protestant denominations, He showed me so many things that should be pointed out to them because many of the Protestants are unaware of their faith's history and of those who began the reformation.

The Lord Jesus asked me, "Do you want to belong to the Church I created in love or to the ones man founded in frustration?" I answered, "Of course Your Church of love." He said, "Well, then, you must be Catholic because this is the Church I gave to mankind through Peter and the authority and power I gave to Peter resides with each of his successors, nowhere else. The completeness of My truth on earth is Catholicism."

I asked the Lord once about our Protestant brothers and sisters. I asked, "There are many that really love You. They have a strong faith and they are really powerful in their faith at times but they do not accept the Eucharist. Will they go to heaven as well?" He said, "Of course, many of them will because they live the faith that they know and so they are judged to that." However, The Lord said it is important that we bring our Protestant brothers and sisters to the true faith, to the fullness of Christianity on earth which is Catholicism which is the Eucharist.

So, there are not only Catholics going to heaven. There will be Muslims, Jews, Hindus, Protestants, and all sorts of people because in many of the other faiths some of the truth of God does reside there, but not in the completeness as it is in Catholicism. So if those people live to the fullness of God as they know it without committing mortal sin then heaven can be theirs.

When Jesus came to me and if He had said, I should be a Protestant, a Hindu, a Jew, well that is what I would have been. He didn't, Jesus said, "Be a Catholic." He said, "This is the faith I gave to mankind. The faith created by God." He explained that the other Christian denominations were created by man and He asked, "Do you want to follow God or man?" I chose God.

The Lord said it is our duty to spread the full truth of God to the world and not to be ashamed or afraid to do so. Today, many Catholics are looking for ecumenism, for unity, but frequently when we look for unity, we are prepared to give some of our faith away. Such as: not to be so obedient to the Church, to its teachings, not to have a full belief in all the sacraments or not to accept the authority or the infallibility of the Pope. When we do that, we are no longer Catholic, we become Protestant because now we are changing and are protesting against what God has given to us. Yes, we must look for unity, we must reach out to all people in love, welcoming them into our Catholic Church because it is the Church for everyone. When the Protestants come back to the Catholic Church, they will bring a richness with them. A richness of community, of understanding of Scripture, a richness of charismatic gifts and they can make our Church stronger. However, we must remember to welcome them in the truth that is Catholicism and not to change that truth and we must never be afraid to stand up and proclaim the complete truth of God on earth.

When I began to speak to Protestants, of course, they had lots of questions. Questions about faith and as I looked to the history of Martin Luther, I found it very easy to answer even if at times the answers were not accepted. In his letter, Let Your Sins Be Strong, Luther said that it is alright to kill a hundred people a day or to commit adultery a hundred times a day, as long as you cling to Christ you will be saved. But that opposes what Christ said in Holy Scripture, He tells us not to sin.

When Luther stated, you are saved by faith alone and not by works, the word "alone" wasn't in original Holy Scripture, it was added by Martin Luther. Also in Saint Matthew's gospel (7:21) Jesus states: "Not everyone who says to me 'Lord, Lord' will enter the kingdom of heaven, but only the one who does the will of my Father in heaven. Many will say to me on that day, 'Lord, Lord did we not prophecy in your name? Did we not drive out demons in your name? Did we not do mighty deeds in your name?' Then I will declare to them solemnly, 'I never knew you. Depart from me you evil doers.'"

Jesus also explains (Matthew 25:34–46), that it was those who turned to the hungry and fed them, thirsty and gave them drink, a stranger and welcomed them, the naked and clothed them, the ill and cared for them, those in prison and visited them. It is these who are righteous and these who are saved. ('what ever you did for these least brothers of mine you did for me'). God is telling us there, do works, good works, because it is faith and works combined, united in love of God and in love of fellow man that brings us to salvation in Christ, Our Lord. Good works are our faith in action. He also states that those who did not do these works '"will go off to eternal punishment but the righteous to eternal life."

Look at what Martin Luther did, there was a prince who was married, and Martin Luther wanted his support. So the prince who was very lustful, said, "If you let me have two wives, I will become Protestant." Martin Luther and another minister married the prince to a second wife while he remained married to the first. After which Luther said to the other minister, "If anyone asks you about this, lie about it." He did not want it known that he had approved and performed a bigamous marriage!

84

Some Protestants believe in predestination (Calvin). That God has selected each person to go to heaven or to go to hell and it does not matter what a person does in their lives. This permits people to commit sin as some believe their sins change nothing. Also this is a denial of Our Lord, Jesus Christ's sacrifice on the cross for if we are predestined there is no reason for His sacrifice as it changes nothing. It too is a denial of Christ's offer of salvation to all.

So there is nothing to fear in speaking to our Protestant brothers and sisters. If we look at their faith, it is very easy to find so many wrongs that many of them do not know about themselves. While if we look at our faith, we can find so many truths to share with them. Read Holy Scripture and your catechism and you have all you need. Then in Christ's love, go out in love and embrace everyone, trying to bring them to Catholicism. That is your duty, and it is a duty of love. Something you should desire to do and when I found that desire, God poured everything into my life needed to do so.

Holy Scripture

The saints told me if I truly wanted to embrace Jesus, that I had to embrace Catholicism. That the Catholic Church is the Body of Christ and so to embrace Jesus, I must embrace the Catholic Church. Through embracing the Church, I would find the guidelines, the help I need to walk the way of Jesus. That the Holy Spirit, working through the Church, unravelled Holy Scripture for mankind and that in the catechism of the Church, He gave us clear guidance on how to live the way of Holy Scripture, the way of Jesus today.

Today many Catholics ask, "How can I live my faith?" I think, maybe people have been blinded a bit. It should be obvious to everyone. You live your faith by living to Holy Scripture and the interpretation of it by the Church in the holy catechism. Here in Holy Scripture and in the holy catechism, the Holy Spirit speaks to us and tells us how to live. The problem is that many Catholics do not have the catechism, and if they have it, they do not read it. No wonder they are confused.

So often I ask Catholics, "Do you have a Bible?" Most of them say, "Yes." I ask, "Do you read it?" They reply, "Occasionally." Some say,

"Every day." And I say, "Do you have a catechism?" Most say, "No." To the few who say they have it, I ask, "Do you read it?" Often they say, "Oh, well, occasionally, very rarely. I do not have time to read it." How foolish that is! In Holy Scripture, there is the Word of God. In the catechism, there is the Holy Spirit through the Church, explaining to us today how to live to the Holy Word of God. Showing us all the things we need to know and how to confront the errors, the sins in the world today. So Holy Scripture and the catechism, they work together. Every one of you should have a catechism, every one of you should be reading it and combining it with Holy Scripture.

It is then you will have a strong faith and when you combine that with a sacramental life, with the Eucharist, then your faith is undefeatable! With this strong faith you can go out and confront anyone and bring anyone to God in love, with the fullness of His truth. That is what we are meant to do! We are not meant to leave other people just praising, worshipping and adoring God and reading the Holy Word. We are meant to bring them to the fullness of faith, the fullness of truth, the fullness of God in the Eucharist so that they can find a full, a happy, a complete life in Him as well. We are not meant to keep it to ourselves. However, due to of lack of knowledge and because of fear and insecurity, many do not do what we are meant to do. So I encourage every one of you, get a catechism. Read it and come to understand your faith.

As I began to read catechism and Holy Scripture, things started to become so clear. At the same time, heaven was helping me to try and live the way of Jesus. The residents of heaven said, "If you want to be Christian, if you want to be Catholic which is the fullness of Christianity, you must live the way of Jesus. As you look to Holy Scripture, see how He lived and try to follow His footsteps because being a Christian is being an imitator of Christ."

— *Understanding Scripture*
When I started to read Holy Scripture without asking the Holy Spirit, I got many different understandings, and so many of them were wrong. I could change Scripture to suit anything, I could find any passage to justify any sin and I wondered why I could do that. The

86

Holy Spirit explained, "Look at when the apostles walked with Jesus. They spent all day with Him. They heard His Holy Word, they saw His wonders. They experienced the Last Supper, the crucifixion, the resurrection. Still they did not properly understand His Holy Word until Pentecost when the Holy Spirit came upon them and showed them the truth." He said, "If it was like that for the apostles who walked with Jesus, it is going to be like that for you and for every person. It is important you recognise that you need God's help to understand Holy Scripture."

So I started to ask the Holy Spirit every time I read Holy Scripture to help me and then the words became so clear. Holy Scripture was entirely different, for it came alive. The words were jumping out from the page and every passage in Holy Scripture, to my surprise, confirmed Catholicism. The Lord said to me, "Also, when you read Holy Scripture, to fully understand it, you must look to the Catholic Church and to read her interpretation of Holy Scripture because the Church is filled with My Holy Spirit. When the Church teaches Holy Scripture to you, it is My Holy Spirit doing it through the Body of Christ."

It seems a lot of Catholics do not do that. They make their own interpretation of Holy Scripture and then surprisingly can change Holy Scripture to suit anything. We can make almost every wrong seem right by Holy Scripture and all because we rely on our humanity and on our pride. We can see the price of that in the Protestant denominations whose faith is based on Martin Luther who misunderstood and confused Scripture. *Now there are 20,000 different denominations, all with different understandings of Holy Scripture when in truth, there is only one true understanding, that is the Catholic one.*

So many people read Holy Scripture and rely on their own interpretation, an interpretation that so often is wrong because we interpret it to suit us, to suit our life in the world. We do not look at the Holy Word with spiritual sight. Doing so brings many different interpretations of the same word, and many different beliefs under the name of Christianity, and all because we have relied on our human self rather than turning to the Holy Spirit to understand the Holy Word of God.

— The Holy Spirit of truth

In everything in our life, in our faith, we must turn to the Holy Spirit and ask for His help. It is when we do that, we start to see the truth and like me, so many will be surprised that the truth is very different from what we think.

The Lord Jesus showed me when He walked the earth, how there were so many synagogues around and many good people, many good Jews went there to pray, to worship God, to read Holy Scriptures, to praise, to adore God. Then He showed me the Temple and He explained this was the only place where the Sacrifice took place. He said, "Today the other Christian denominations are the synagogues, full of people praising, loving, worshipping God. However, there is only one Church where the Sacrifice takes place and that is the Catholic Church and if you want to be close to Me and filled with Me, you must come and celebrate the Sacrifice." The Lord said it is the duty of everyone in the temple to bring those in the synagogues to celebrate the sacrifice of the Eucharist.

The Lord said, "Do not be blinded by the world and by clever arguments. Ask My Holy Spirit to show you the truth in Holy Scripture." As I looked to Holy Scriptures in that way it came alive and I saw the divine truth of the Catholic Church. Sadly many Catholics are afraid to proclaim their faith and so often that fear comes from not knowing the faith. Usually when people learn about it, they learn about it with human eyes and understanding rather than asking the Holy Spirit to teach them. If they would learn through the Holy Spirit they would have no fear. Catholics would stand up gently but firmly, lovingly but kindly, sharing the fullness of God's love with everyone. Knowing that Holy Scripture would back them up.

Sacrifice and service

In life today for many people, service and sacrifice are dirty words instead of the blessed words that they truly are. We have been blinded by the world to think of self and we can see the results – families falling apart, marriages falling apart, society falling apart.

So many marriages fall apart because of selfishness. In marriage, a husband is meant to serve and to sacrifice for his wife. Just as the wife is meant to serve and sacrifice for her husband. It is when you are living the marriage in this way that the marriage will be strong because as you sacrifice in that way, you imitate Jesus Christ's sacrificial love and you invite Him into your marriage.

It is the same for families, when they sacrifice one for another, they are inviting Christ into their family in their sacrifice and He strengthens the family.

When you live marriage in sacrifice, then Jesus is there strongly uniting husband and wife. Then the husband and wife together sacrifice and serve the children. This is the love that is meant to be in families. Unfortunately because so many are self-centred, it is not that way and so marriages are falling apart. No wonder society is falling apart because marriages and families are the cornerstones of society and how the evil one laughs at how easily he has got us focused on self and he is destroying our very society. If only Catholics would live the faith as Jesus calls us to, the one that calls for sacrificial love and not a self-centred love. We in our foolishness keep embracing evil, if we would instead embrace the cross of Jesus and carry His cross with us in our hearts wherever we go, then His victory over evil is with us and there is nothing evil can do to us. To carry that cross, it has to be a cross of love, loving God, loving others and preparing to sacrifice for God and for others, just as Jesus did. It is through that divine cross of love that we are delivered from evil.

It seems some Catholics do not want to sacrifice for others. They do not mind others sacrificing for them, but so often, when they have to sacrifice something, they do not want to do it. Yet sacrifice is an essential part to our faith. Our faith is built on the sacrificial love of Christ, Our Lord. Each of the sacraments is full of sacrificial love but often people are blind to that. No wonder society is so empty, so loveless. If we do not live the sacrificial way of Christ, how can we expect His love to reach out through the world?

We should not just expect the priests and the religious to sacrifice and serve. We are the Body of Christ, Our sacrificial Lord, and as part of that Body, we are supposed to sacrifice. It is when you sacrifice for Christ and for others, through your efforts, He opens your heart, your soul, in a special way. He reaches inside of you and gives you the grace, the strength, to carry any cross, to endure anything in love of Him and love of others.

When heaven first came to me, I was told I must sacrifice if I want to be Christian because to be a Christian is to be an imitator of Christ. When Jesus came to earth, He showed us in His life how we were to live. His life was one of total service and sacrifice. He served the Father in everything, He served everyone, putting others before Himself. He sacrificed for the Father and sacrificed for mankind, putting Himself last, even putting Himself in the lowest position.

So if I am to be like Christ, I must sacrifice. That is how we are meant to live and so every day I pray for the grace to be able to do so. As imitators of Christ we are meant to put God first in all things and to put others before ourselves and to put ourselves last. It is when we put ourselves last that God puts us first. It is when we are prepared to sacrifice for God and for others in love that truly we open ourselves to God's divine grace because the main barriers between man and God are pride and selfishness. When you put God first and others before yourself, the barrier of self is destroyed. When you are prepared to sacrifice for others, pride is destroyed and then, in humble love, you are open completely to God.

You come to see that by serving others and by sacrificing for others, you please God. Now when you leave the church and go out into the world, you no longer expect the world to do everything for you but you expect to do everything for the world desiring to change the world for the better and finding it is in sacrificial love that you can. Now when you leave the Eucharist in this way, you do not leave Christ behind but He comes with you. He is living inside you just as you are living in Him, with Him and through Him.

Every step you take He is taking with you. Every good thing you try to do He is doing with you, every act of sacrifice, of love and of service, He is doing with you. Every cross you have to carry, and there are many, He carries with you and for you. It is when you live this way, living for Christ not only in the church but also out in the world, you truly live your Catholic faith. When a billion Catholics live their Eucharistic faith within the Church and outside of the Church, then the light of Christ will shine so brightly in the world that darkness will flee and paradise will come to earth. It begins with each one of you, not someone else, living your Eucharistic, your sacrificial and your serving faith. This is the faith that Christ calls us to. Are we going to answer that call?

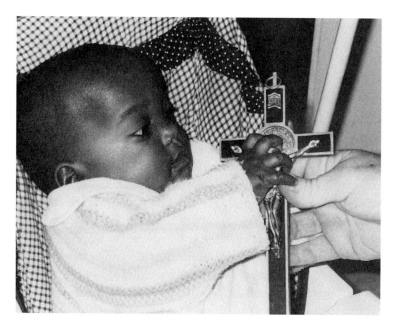

The sign of the cross

In my pride, I thought I knew all about prayer. But heaven decided to show me another way to pray. It is in the sign of the cross. In this prayer, the saints told me how to focus on sacrifice.

I would come into the church and make the sign of the cross or when I began to pray but I did not think much about it. It was just something I did before I started to pray. However, heaven showed me that the sign of the cross is a deeply spiritual prayer, or is meant to be, that will bring you to focus on sacrifice. That the sign of the cross is the sign of God's love for you and it should be the sign of your love for God and when you make that sign you should be looking heavenward, looking to God.

— *In the name of the Father*

When you say, "In the name of the Father," look to your divine Father in heaven. Ask the Holy Spirit to help you let your mind be lifted heavenwards. Thinking of how much God loves you that He sent His only Son to suffer and die on the cross to reconcile heaven and earth, to carry the weight of your sins, to suffer in life for you. Look to the divine and unconditional love of the Father, the love He has for you and for every person. His love in all He gives you in your life and in the world around you. See how much He wants to help you in your life. Call out to the Father that you love Him and that truly, He is your Father. You should be calling out for His love, longing for His love, desiring to be closer and closer to Him. Desiring that your mind through His grace may be lifted to Him.

As you think of the Father, think of His heart on the cross. "In the name of the Father," is meant to take your heart, your soul, reaching out in love to the Father, calling out, "Father, Abba, I love You, and I thank You for the depth of Your love, that You would love someone like me, that You would think of someone like me, that You would allow a sinner like me to exist."

When I say, "In the name of the Father," I should think that He truly is my Father. That He made us all His children and so when I lift my thoughts heavenward to the Father, I should not only be lifting my self to God in heaven, but lifting everyone else who is a child of God to heaven.

— *In the name of Jesus*

When I place my hand on the stomach, 'and of the Son,' to think how much Jesus loved me that He would suffer and die for me, a weak sinner. That He would lower Himself to come to earth, that He would endure torment, torture, suffering, for me and for all, because He loves us, and for no other reason except He loves us.

Realising also that when I place my hand on my stomach, that just as my body needs feeding, so does my soul. That Jesus once again in His divine humble love, lowers Himself to be the food for my weak human soul so that it can grow in His grace and that my spirit can be strong in His spirit.

Jesus in the Eucharist is the Food, He is the divine Drink that your soul thirsts for, hungers for. Realising as you receive Him within, in that receiving, you receive His divine sacrifice for in every Eucharist is His death, His resurrection.

"And of the Son," thinking of how He hung on the cross, how He opened His flesh for you, for all of us. How He opened His tender heart in love and poured out His divine grace, His divine mercy for all mankind. How in agony, He cried out His love for us and offered us an eternal embrace of love. Think of Jesus opening His arms on the cross and calling out, "I love you, and it does not matter how much you hurt Me, still I love you."

When you place your hand on your stomach, "And of the Son," to think of how He still suffers when you sin as you make the cross weigh more upon Him, when you continue to wound Him. That those five wounds are bleeding and bleeding because of the sins we do. But then seeing by the power of the Holy Spirit that your love for Christ, your love for the Father, your love for the Holy Spirit comforts the Lord in His suffering as He bathes His holy wounds in our love.

— *In the name of the Holy Spirit*

Saying, 'And the Holy Spirit,' knowing that the Holy Spirit will fill your spirit through the grace and sacrifice of Jesus, to give you the strength to carry any cross, to endure any sacrifice for the love of God and for the love of others. Seeing any cross that would be put upon you would not be a curse, it would be a blessing. Knowing in that blessing, the Holy Spirit would pour out His strength, His power to fill your spirit with the fire of His love, to live the faith in loving crosses, in carrying crosses.

When praying, 'And of the Holy Spirit,' to think how Jesus and the Father sent the Holy Spirit to earth to bless us all and to help us. To think of the gifts and of the graces that the Holy Spirit offers everyone and how the Holy Spirit, because He loves us, just because He loves us, will give us the strength to shoulder any cross.

Then realising that the Holy Spirit would lift your soul, lift your mind to God and then you realise in the Holy Spirit, your humanity is lifted to heaven by His divine love, His divine grace. Seeing how the

Holy Spirit will fill our human spirit with His Divine Spirit and lift us and fill us with all that we need to live our faith.

Think of how in the Eucharist, heaven and earth are united in Jesus by the grace of the Holy Spirit.

— *The sign of the cross and the passion*
When you are making that sign of the cross, see Jesus on the cross before you. See how much He loved you that He would come to earth, would be tortured, would be abused and would be put to death for your sins. Yet never did He complain, all He did was reach out in love and offer forgiveness. So when you suffer, when you make that sign of the cross, offer your suffering to Jesus on the cross without complaining about your suffering, without blaming God for your suffering. See that no matter how much you suffer, Jesus suffered more. As you offer your suffering up to Him on the cross, allow Him to draw you up on the cross with Him. That is what He did to me once.

As He drew me onto the cross, I experienced some of the agony, it would be impossible for me to experience all of it, and I experienced ecstasy. I saw how through His suffering, Jesus was filled with ecstasy as He looked throughout time and He saw all the souls that would be saved by His suffering and that brought Him such deep joy. It is when you offer your suffering to Jesus on the cross in this way, you will find that through your suffering, Jesus will offer you joy, will offer you happiness as you see that Jesus draws your suffering into His. How He allows your suffering to become part of His act of salvation and that brings the deepest joy as you realise, through your suffering, souls are saved by the grace of God.

That sign of the cross is a beautiful spiritual prayer if we say it in love and ask the Holy Spirit to show us the cross and Jesus on the cross.

— *The five wounds of Christ*
When you make that sign of the cross and you see your five fingers, think of the five wounds of Christ. How He shed His blood for you. How He poured out His love for you through each holy wound. How He accepted that pain, how He endured that torture for our sins. When you place your hand on your head, think of how Christ was wounded

for you, how He suffered for you. Think of how He only showed love, and for that He suffered. Think of how He opened His flesh for you and for all of us, so that His precious Blood would flow over the world and wash us in His divine love.

Think of how you hurt Him with your sins, of how you wound Him. But then think of how Jesus opened His heart in forgiving love for everyone, no matter what they have done.

Then as you go out to the world as a Catholic, sharing your faith, realise just as Christ suffered for His love, you may suffer for yours. Also, see that just as Christ was wounded on the cross for living the truth, that you, too, when you live your truth in the Catholic faith, at times you would be wounded by others as they make fun of you, as they abuse you, as they reject you. As they may even hurt and kill you but do not be afraid of that. Welcome it! See if that happens you are truly imitating Christ. So, like Christ, do not be afraid to live the truth, to live love, because when you do that, in Christ, you become by His grace, Jesus to the world.

When you reach out to others to help them, every time think of the five wounds of Christ and see how He was wounded for everyone else, not just for you. Understand also that when you reach out to others, that when you truly imitate Christ, then at times you would be wounded, you would be hurt but do not let that stop you. Realise it is through your sacrifices God gives you so many graces and gifts to bless your life, your family life and the world.

Think of how through the suffering of Christ, so much grace was poured out onto the world. How, if you are wounded, if you are hurt for Christ, as you reach out in love to others, then God will pour grace out through you to touch the world. Think what a blessing that is! Because when you do that, Christ lifts you up onto the cross with Him. He embraces you in His divine suffering love, and as you offer Him your wounds, your hurt, by His grace, you unite in His act of salvation and become part of that act of salvation and what a blessing that is!

Then, every time as you reach out to someone, with the five fingers in your hand, see the wounds of Christ reaching out and desire to sacrifice as Christ sacrificed. Accepting that at times you will be wounded, you will be hurt when you try to live the way of Christ. For if you try to love as Christ loved, if you try to open your heart to all people as you are meant to, in tender love, in gentle love, in sacrificial love, then often people will respond in ways that will hurt you. For that is the way they responded to Christ, Our Lord.

If we are to imitate Him, we should expect that and realise, when this happens, that is a wonderful blessing. Because as you are reaching out in the love of Christ united in your love, thinking of the sacrificial love, the sacrificial wounds of Christ, then evil will get angry as it got angry with Christ. You then realise, that when people hurt you, when people abuse you, make fun of you, for trying to love as Christ loved, then you know you are doing right, you are doing good. You understand that evil is angry with you because you are united with Christ in His suffering, in His sacrificial love.

When you come to see that, you no longer fear being abused, being rejected or being hurt. When it happens, you just thank God for it and for those who have hurt you and just as Christ does, you have a deep desire to keep loving them and forgiving them. This is the Catholic way of the cross – the way that so many reject because sacrifice has become a dirty word.

— *Jesus going out to others with you*
When you reach out to the poor, to the needy, as you are meant to, reach out and see your hand is the wounded hand of Christ that is pouring out love to them. Go to them with the wounded heart of Christ that opens itself wide and says, "I love you. No matter who you are, no matter what you have done."

As He poured His love out to those in need through His wounds, then you reach out to others in love and embrace them as the wounded Christ, so you can bring them to a full and joyful life in Him.

It is when you do this, when you see the sinner, the one who does the most terrible sins, you no longer condemn or judge them. Then you start to see them as Christ sees them, with the forgiving and loving eyes of Christ. You realise they are just weak humans who are trapped by evil, who have succumbed to evil and you have the desire to help them out of the grasp of evil. Your heart and soul aches to set them free from that evil through love, through prayers, through sacrifice.

As you go to those who are sick and who are poor, no longer do you turn away from them, because you are not thinking of self. No, you reach out to those who are sick no matter what sickness they have. Now you want to embrace them and love them because that is what Christ does from the cross.

Now you never you look down on the poor because they have nothing. Instead you start to feel ashamed of yourself because you have so much and there is a burning desire to share all you have with the poor and needy because in them, you see our suffering Lord.

The sign of the cross is a deeply spiritual prayer which can lift you to mystical levels that you could never imagine if you ask the Holy Spirit to show you the depth of this sign. As you do that, you come to see that YOU are meant to be the sign of the cross for the world. Today, many Catholics are looking for signs and wonders while you are meant to be the sign, you are meant to be the wonder. You are meant to be the sign of Jesus and the wonder of His love, going out to the world and allowing His grace to pour through you, to change your family, to change your friends, to change you. To change the world so it can be a better place.

So many Catholics complain about how bad the world is and sit back and do nothing. How can you expect the world to change if *you* do nothing? It is when a billion Catholics stand up and proclaim the love of Christ, live as His sign, live as His wonder, live as His love, that is when the world will change and be a better place.

The sign of the cross is the most wonderful, spiritual sign, a deep loving prayer for me now as it should be for all people. However, many Catholics, when they make that holy sign, they are too busy thinking about themselves, thinking about their lives, so easily distracted, so that they do not allow the grace of God to lift them heavenward through this divine sign.

For me, the sign of the cross has become a very special prayer and every time I make that sign of the cross, that sign of God's love for me, the sign of His love for everyone, I realise it must be my sign of my love for God.

Through that sign I now call out to Jesus, offering Him every moment of joy in my life, every moment of happiness, every moment of love, offering it to Him on the cross in His suffering, so that by His grace, in some way, it may comfort Him. I also offer Him all my suffering and in that offering, I thank Him for my suffering because I see what a blessing suffering is. Because when you return your suffering as an offering of love to Jesus, He lifts that suffering up to the cross with Him, unites it in His suffering and so it becomes part of His act of salvation for mankind.

Suffering

When I started to make the sign of the cross in this way I began to see Jesus suffering on the cross before me and I realised that His pain was caused by my sins. Every sin I did was hurting Jesus but still, through His pain, through His suffering, gently He called out that He loved me. He said to me, "In your life, offer your suffering to Me." So I began to offer all my pain and my hurt and my struggles to Him.

When I was first shown this, when I saw Jesus suffering and dying on the cross, I now had a strong desire inside me to offer all my suffering to Jesus. As I did, He lifted me one day on the cross with Him. I saw how much Jesus suffered for us because He loves us and now I had a desire to offer Him more and more suffering. This was because Jesus showed me that when we offer our suffering to Him on the cross, when we offer it in love of Him and of others, and not offer it in expectation for something for ourselves, then we imitate Jesus and are showing sacrificial love. He then lifts our suffering up to the cross and unites it with His suffering, to pour out grace over the world, to touch hearts and souls and convert them.

What a blessing that is that through our suffering, others may be saved! Now I cannot stop thanking God even in those moments when I hurt so much, when it is such a struggle, by the grace of God I turn to God and thank Him and ask Him for the grace to endure anything. He fills me with joy, with peace, with happiness through my suffering which He will do for any of you because He loves you the same as He loves me. Instead of making your suffering a cross for yourself, turn to Jesus and offer it to Him in love on the cross and find your suffering becomes truly a blessing.

Some people see suffering as a curse. It is only a curse if you make it that way. When you offer it to God in love, then it truly becomes a blessing because He pours joy into your heart in your suffering, He gives you the strength to endure anything and to do it joyfully, in love of God and of fellow man. Sadly so many Catholics do not understand this. For some it is so easy to feel self-pity and become self-centred in their pain as they say, "Why has God given me this suffering," and they blame Him saying, "Why am I suffering and not someone else?" Why would you want someone to suffer like you do? What a terrible thing!

You know, I meet many dying people in agony and there are two types. There are those who are focused on self and it is very difficult to be around them. They are so miserable, so unhappy, and they become a burden on everyone.

Then there are those who love God. In their suffering, in their hurt, even in their death, they are joyful. It is in these people you can truly see Christ, Our Lord and it is such a blessing to be near them. It makes you feel happy. Suffering is not a curse, for those who love Christ it is a blessing!

I remember a Fr. Sean Sorahan who was a priest that first helped me. I used to visit him when he was dying of cancer. Fr Sean was in terrible pain; at times the pain was almost unbearable. Yet through his pain he was happy, he was full of joy. He did not lose his sense of humour and would still make me laugh with his jokes. Also he was waiting, with great anticipation, for the day he would die so that he would see Jesus. This priest was a fine example on how to endure pain and how to die joyfully in the love of God.

Purity and marriage

To be a Christian is to be an image of Christ, an imitator of Christ. Christ who is pure love and each one of you is called to a pure life in Christ. It is through that pure life, God pours divine grace into your hearts, into your souls and gives you all you need in life.

— Impurity

The world draws us into impurity. For many Catholics, purity is a dirty word or it is something they ignore or they think is impossible to achieve. We have impure thoughts, about ourselves, about others. We say at times impure words and do impure actions and the world including many Catholics even laugh at purity. Many people think purity is a stupid word. How the evil one has blinded us! Purity is a wonderful word! It is when we seek to live pure lives in Christ, Our Lord, we open our lives, our hearts and our souls to God and allow His grace to come into us and fill our lives. The purer we are, then the more grace comes into us because there are less barriers between us and God. It is in purity we can become more like Jesus. Also it is in purity we can experience full and true love.

God calls us in Holy Scripture to be perfect, to try to be pure in Him. Now, as humans, that is very hard because we are imperfect. We are weak, we are fragile, and it is so easy to be drawn into the ways of the world. But to live that pure life is what each of us should be seeking. So many of us are not because we are looking in the wrong direction. We are meant to be looking beyond the world in our life, in our faith but today, for many Catholics, their faith is worldly. They change their faith to suit the world, to suit themselves. When they look at the Church and look at the sacraments, they look with worldly eyes and because of that, they miss so much in their faith and in their life. We are meant to look beyond the world, we are meant to look to God in heaven with a spiritual sight, with a mystical sight – sight that we can find through the Church, which is the mystical Body of Christ. In His mystical Body, He will lift our thoughts heavenward. He will lift us beyond the desires of the world to desire the eternal joyful life in heaven. In the sacraments, He will give us the way of finding that pure life we are meant to live.

Of course, in baptism, our soul is purified as we die to self and come to a pure life in Christ, but God knows how weak we are and He knows we will fall down and do impure things. So He gives us the wonderful sacrament of confession where we can open our heart to God in love and allow His Holy Spirit through the priest to purify our soul when we have a complete confession.

While in the sacrament of the Eucharist, the divine Lord, the pure One, will come into us and fill us with His purity and if we allow Him to, He will purify our body, our soul, our mind, in Him. He fills us with His purity hoping that we will embrace that purity in our lives. He will give us the strength to live His way, to try to live a pure life, in pure love. Then, just as He looked to the Father with pure thoughts in His life, He will give us the grace to do the same in ours.

In your everyday life, you can be pure in Christ; pure life is not impossible. You only have to desire it, to seek it, to want it and when you receive that grace, then inside you, every moment your heart, your very soul will be dancing with joy.

— *Marriage*

In marriage, in that beautiful sacrament, here, physical and emotional love becomes pure in Christ, Our Lord. When God is invited into the marriage and embraced in every moment, then the love in the marriage becomes pure, becomes strong.

When you truly love God and put Him first in your life, then He comes first in your marriage. So then in your marriage, all you want to do is love God, adore God and worship God and you realise you can do that by having a pure and sacrificial love in your marriage. It is when you live and experience love in that way, it is beyond any worldly love because you begin to experience the fullness of love.

A lot of people have got love confused. For some people, love is physical. Well, a physical love alone soon becomes lust and leads people to do things they should not do. Many people have lust confused for love, and how the evil one laughs at that! Sadly, so many young people have lust confused with love.

Some people have an emotional love, but in life our emotions change and so often, as they change, our love can be broken. If you only have an emotional and a physical love, it is so easy for your love to die, for it to become impure and for you to be led into doing things you should not do. No wonder so many marriages struggle. No wonder there is so much divorce.

Today many people think they know love but even those who are married and think they are in love often do not experience the

fullness of love because all they are experiencing is the physical and the emotional love. Love is far more than that. Love is spiritual. Love is mystical. Love is eternal. To experience spiritual and mystical love, you have to live in the eternal love of Christ. It is when you live in Christ, Our Lord, in the Eucharist, you experience that spiritual and mystical love and that comes alive in the love of your husband, your wife, your family, your friends.

For now every time you reach out in love, you experience so much joy, so much happiness, so much excitement because in every moment of true love, Jesus is inside you, loving you and through you, others.

In marriage, and in all love, true love is meant to be more than physical, more than emotional. It is meant to be spiritual, it is meant to be mystical. In marriage, when you invite God into your marriage in the sacrament, your marriage becomes a Trinitarian celebration of love with God at the head of the marriage and the husband and the wife making up the trinity. The husband and wife in love of each other, and then their love united in the love of God. Then as their love is united in this way God fills their spirits with His love and brings their love to a deeper, a stronger, purer love. Now they start to experience mystical love in their marriage where they come to know each other in such a deep way, at times they even know each other's thoughts and feelings without words being spoken.

When you live your marriage in a Trinitarian way, with God at the head of your marriage, He draws you to experience that spiritual and mystical love in Him so that love is strong throughout your life and strong in eternity. God pours out mystical gifts in marriage through love, a love that will last forever. Sometimes you see the effect of that pure love, when the husband or the wife die, often in that wonderful love, the other partner dies shortly afterwards showing the power of the union of their love. It is not broken in death but is brought to fullness in God in death for eternity.

It is when you come to the sacraments, you can start to experience the spiritual and mystical love. That is why the sacrament of marriage is such an important sacrament and that is why it is so important that we save ourselves for marriage when we are young.

With Christ invited into every moment of the marriage, this is when people look beyond the physical self, beyond the emotional self. This is when man and woman truly unite to become one in love. As they offer every moment of their marriage to God in love, God pours out His grace and lifts the husband and wife close to Him, bringing His Spirit of love into their hearts and souls. He lifts them beyond the physical, beyond the emotional. Now your heart, your very soul begins to truly love as it is filled with the spiritual and mystical love of God and each other. That is when the husband and wife become one in the fullness of true love and then that sacred love becomes sweet, becomes strong. It becomes unbreakable.

As that love grows to what it should be, then every time a wife sacrifices for her husband or a husband sacrifices for his wife, there is no resentment, there is no anger, there is only happiness that they can show their love in that way. Now they see through their sacrifices, they are imitating the sacrifice of Christ. It is as they sacrifice together in love, offering it to God, that is when the Lord lifts them up to the cross with Him and unites them in His sacrificial love, in His mystical love.

When Christ reaches down from the cross and draws the marriage up onto the cross with Him, He lifts it on high for all to see so that the Catholic marriage becomes a light burning in the dark, an example to all. Yes, I mean, you will still have your arguments and disagreements. Just ask my wife. But despite those, inside you, there is this deep and burning love because now no longer is self first. It is self that destroys marriages. It is sacrifice and love that builds them. Sadly so many Catholic marriages are weak because of self where they should be strong in sacrifice.

In a marriage that is lived in this way of sacrifice and service, the fullness of love is found. So that now when the wife loves the husband, she sees she is loving Christ in him and when the man loves the wife, the man sees he is loving Christ in her. When you keep Christ at the head of the marriage in this way and try to imitate Him, then self is put out of the marriage and so the love grows and grows to become strong. You then experience love in more than a worldly way for you are drawn into the eternal love of God, which lifts you beyond this world. So your marriage is no longer a burden or a difficulty, but in every day you see it as a great blessing. This is how a Catholic marriage is meant to be, full of sacrifice and service and empty of self.

When you feel the sacrificial embrace of Christ, that loving embrace, then finally you know what love truly is. It is not worldly, it is eternal. It is forever and it is only you that changes that by not living a pure and a true life in Christ. Today, so many people deny themselves so much because they will not love as they should. Sacrifice is one of the keys to our faith.

It is so obvious today that many marriages are not marriages in Christ but marriages in self where the husband or the wife put themselves first and expect to be served instead of serving. The husband demanding of the wife or the woman demanding of the husband. Demanding what they want and focused on self. Now they are not looking to Christ, seeing what He wants. That is not how marriage is meant to be.

No wonder marriages fall apart. No wonder, husbands and wives grow to dislike each other, find it hard to talk to each other, find it hard to show true love. When your focus is on self, it closes you to all these things and all because self is first, Christ is forgotten in the marriage and service and sacrifice are not even thought of. Yet still people think they are living a Catholic marriage, which is a sacrament of true love. So, unless you have true love in the sacrament of your marriage, then it is very likely it will fail and to experience the fullness of love is only possible in the body of love, in Our Lord, Jesus Christ.

Spiritual sight

It is when you unite completely with Jesus in the Eucharist, you experience what love truly is. It is eternal, it is glorious, it is blissful.

We are called to look beyond the world, to look to eternity in heaven and when you do this in the Eucharist, you experience the fullness of love, the fullness of Christ and the fullness of life. Even though we may not understand it in our mind, our hearts and our souls dance for joy knowing the fullness of love and our spirit is on fire with love.

As we look at others never again do we look at them feeling hate or feeling resentment. Never again can we stop loving we just want to reach out and embrace them in the heart of Christ, because that full love, that divine love in us drives us to live a life of love. This is the life the saints lived. This is the life you are meant to live. Unfortunately so many people do not and because they live their worldly and self-centred lives, life is so empty and meaningless. How sad it is that many people today do not experience the fullness of love because they are more interested in the fullness of self.

Most of us are unbalanced in our human nature. There are two parts of our nature. There is the physical, human side of us and there is a spiritual side. Most of us live the physical, the human side and we live our faith in that earthly way. When you live that way, then you are drawn away from God and confusion comes into your life. You have to live in balance, live the spiritual way as well, focusing on God then He brings your humanity into balance and for this, you have to be asking the Holy Spirit every day to help you live the right way. When you focus on God in that balanced way and ask for the grace to do so, as you start to live the spiritual life, it brings your human life to fullness. It brings goodness, peace, happiness into your humanity. However, because we are unbalanced, we are trapped in the world, prisoners of the world and we are being drawn away from God. We should be free in God and drawn to Him, and that will bring our life to fullness in Him.

How sad it is that many people, many Christians, many Catholics still think they are living the right way when in fact, they are living the way of everyone else and making excuses for the sins they do and just cling to Jesus and think it is okay. Well, it is not. God calls us to look to heaven, not to look to earth. Every day I pray to the Lord that I can keep my focus on Him because it is so easy to be distracted into the world. When you are on a journey, you are meant to look to the destination you are going to. So if you want to go to heaven, you should look to it. Sadly today, many Catholics have got worldly sight and not a heavenly sight and because of that, when they look at their faith they see it in a worldly way and may not understand it. When we look at our faith, we are meant to look with heavenly eyes, looking for the spiritual and mystical, looking beyond the world.

It is when you discover the spiritual and mystical in this faith, you come to understand that the Catholic faith is unique because you come to understand that truly, the Holy Catholic and Apostolic Church is the Body of Christ. You understand that you are part of this Body and with spiritual and mystical sight you come to realise that every moment you live and in all you do, you are living in Christ and doing all in Christ and that Christ is living in you and is doing good through you.

When you come to understand this, you have the strong desire never to sin again and never to stop loving. Never will you feel hatred again, because when you look upon others, now you look with the eyes of Christ. Now you look with spiritual sight and even when you see the worst sinner, you do not want to condemn them or judge them, you want to help them, as you realise that they are weak humans that are overcome by evil like every one of us can be.

We however, who are the Body of Christ, are graced in a special way. We are graced with the strength to stand against evil. One of those great strengths is that when you see evil, you see evil in others, you do not respond in evil with bad thoughts, with bad words, with condemnation, with judgement, with anger, with resentment. All you do is respond in forgiving love, as you understand, that is how Christ overcame evil and that is how you will, too.

I speak to so many people and they say that when they come to Mass, they find it so empty. They complain that the churches are empty with only five or six people coming along. This only shows that there is a misunderstanding of the Holy Eucharist and that people are not looking properly. The churches are never empty! When you look with spiritual sight by the grace of the Holy Spirit, you start to see what a mystical experience the Eucharist truly is. Today, because so many of us are looking to the world, we are not looking for the mystical experiences in the mystical Body of Christ, which is this Church, in those mystical and mysterious sacraments. When the Holy Spirit opens your eyes to see these things, all of a sudden, you realise that at every Mass, the churches are full! They are full with angels and saints, bowing and worshipping and adoring Our Lord. You start to see that at Holy Mass, there is the whole of heaven celebrating the Eucharist with you. This is where the heavenly Body, the heavenly Church, unites with the earthly Body, with the earthly Church. We become one in Christ, Our Lord and now the Church becomes complete and full in Him. Most people do not see this because they are looking to the world, they are not looking to heaven.

They are not asking the Holy Spirit to open their eyes to see the truth, the power and the majesty of the Eucharist. Due to that, people see so little in it and miss out on these wonderful mystical experiences that are there for all people. We only have to seek them, want them and ask for them by the grace of the Holy Spirit.

Often I am asked by Catholics how can they achieve higher spiritual levels, how can they get higher graces, how can they improve their spiritual life and maybe have some mystical experiences? Often they are looking for signs and wonders. Many go looking for visions and go to many holy places, which of course can build the faith up but many Catholics have forgotten the basics of our faith, the basics that open us up to the mystical experiences and love of God.

Jesus said, "The two greatest commandments are to love God with your whole heart, your whole mind, your whole body, your whole being, and then to love others as I love you, as you love yourself."

These two commandments are the greatest commandments. This is what our faith is built on and this is what our life should be built on. Jesus said very clearly in Holy Scripture that everything else is built on these two commandments.

— *The first commandment – to love God*

Often these seem too simple for many Catholics and they think so little of them and look for more complicated things. Yet, it is these two commandments that open up your life to God, open up your faith to you, bring you a deeper spiritual life and lift you to higher levels of grace. It is by living these two commandments, you start to discover the true spiritual and mystical world in the Catholic Church.

It is when you give yourself totally to God in the first commandment, every day saying to Him, "I am Yours, God, all of me. I love You above all others, even above myself. You are everything, Lord, I live for You." It is when you say this and truly mean this that your heart opens wide to God and you are drawn into the truth of our Catholic faith. It is then that you are loving God in a total giving of self to Him in love and it is through doing your best to live that way that you are lifted to higher graces and to higher gifts.

It is when you give yourself completely to God in love and embrace His love completely into your life that now you live as God created you to. God created us to be in His image and His image is the image of love. So we must be love and we must try and have the same love that God has which is an unconditional love. God just loves us unconditionally. He does not demand anything from us. He asks us to live the right way, so that we can have happy lives on earth and live eternally in His joy.

Also when we come to God and love Him, we are meant to come with a total giving of self and demanding nothing. So many people come to God and say, "I love You if You give me this or You will do this for me." When they do not get what they want or something goes wrong, they maybe get angry with God or turn from God. How foolish that is. God does not love us that way, He never turns away from us.

If you can imitate God's love with that total giving of self to Him, then you will find everything opens up to you. That you are drawn into the Catholic Church is to be expected because this is the loving Body of Christ and so in giving ourselves to God we give ourselves to His Body.

It is when you give yourself totally to God and do this every day, living totally for Him and thanking Him for the wonderful gift He has given to you in your life by returning that gift to Him, that your faith and your life find fullness. Once you are living for God, the Church, sacraments and prayer open up and so does life on earth because now as you live completely for God, in every moment you experience His love. In a blade of grass you see His love, in the plants, the trees, in the animals, in each other you see the gift of God's love. When you feel the wind on your face, you feel the breath of God's love. Now all around you, you see God everywhere and His love everywhere.

Today so many are blind in their faith, blinded by self and the world, instead of having the spiritual sight that God wants to give in love. When you love God completely and give Him every moment of your life in love, truly inviting God into your life as master and not as your servant and when you desire to serve and please Him in everything you do, that is when your faith opens up.

You see what a treasure your Catholic faith is, what a treasure your Church is. Now you realise this truly is the Body of Christ and you realise if you want to totally give yourself to God, then you must live in the Church, in its fullness.

— *The second commandment – to love one another*
As you see that the most important thing is to love God and find eternal life in Him you realise you could spend your whole life meditating on this first commandment and never understand it completely.

It also becomes obvious that the second commandment comes from the first commandment because if you love God completely, you cannot help but love others because you see each person as a creation of God's love. You see how God loves and treasures each one and now you have to do the same because you love God and in your love, you desire only to please Him and to please Him, you know, is to love others. It does not matter any more how tall or how short people are, how skinny or how fat they are, how rich or how poor they are, now you just love everyone because you realise this is how God loves them. You realise this is what Jesus showed you in His life. You cannot stop thanking God for each person and you find joy in each person. When you look with eyes of love, you see the beauty of God's love in every person. It becomes impossible to dislike anyone, impossible to hate anyone. Even when you see the people doing the worst possible sins, all you feel is pity and sorrow for them as you see how evil has worked on their weaknesses to draw them into the dark. In love of God and in love of others you ache and long to pray for them, you feel such a deep sorrow and you want them to come into the light of God's love.

In your love of God and of others, you desire only to humble yourself before God and before others. Now you only want to serve God and serve others and it is then that your soul truly opens wide to be drawn into your Catholic faith as you embrace it with eyes of love, not eyes of self, eyes that are focused on God and not on the world.

Now you realise that every sacrament is a gift of God's sacrificial love where He offers us the opportunity to come closer to Him, to be purified by Him, to be filled with Him and to be drawn up to such high levels of grace you could never imagine. It is in the sacraments you can find the higher graces, the higher gifts because in every sacrament is the presence and love of God, the gifts and graces of God. You realise it is through the sacraments that you can come closer and closer to Him and eventually can become one with Him.

— *Love and confession*
Living this way, you have a burning desire to be as close to God as you can and you realise that is only possible through the sacraments where God is present in all His glory. In the sacraments you now see the gifts of God's love. In every sacrament you see the power of His love, the presence of His love, the pure sacrificial love of Jesus. No longer are the sacraments a duty or a routine that you do, but you come willingly, you come with a desire to truly partake in the sacraments and now you have a longing, an ache to partake of the sacraments frequently.

You have a desire to come to confession frequently because you realise how powerful a gift confession is. Now, by the grace of God, in humble love, you recognise your weaknesses and you see how even through the smallest sin, you hurt God and how you hurt others and yourself. As you are trying to live each moment for God, as you are trying to achieve perfection in Him, you see how often you stumble, in pride, in self. You realise how often you fall down through little or big sins but then you see the glory of God's love in the sacrament of reconciliation. You realise in this wonderful sacrament the Lord is calling out to you, "Come to Me, no matter what you have done. Come to Me and let Me purify your soul. Let Me lift you up when you fall down. Let Me fill you with My grace, My strength, My gifts. Let Me make you pure so that you can receive Me in the way you should."

As you do not want to offend God, you come to confession in humble love and bow down opening your heart completely to Him, crying out for His forgiveness. Now your soul drives you to the sacrament of reconciliation because it wants to be purified and cleansed from the stains of sin. So in love you come and open your heart to God and say, "Forgive me, I am sorry." God answers, "Of course, I forgive you."

You would not hold any sins back. Sometimes people hold back the really bad sins because they are ashamed of those but in true love, there is no shame, there is no embarrassment. In true love you would open your heart and know that God will forgive you because He loves you. He understands your weaknesses and in love, He does not want to condemn you, He wants to help you. Now you would see confession as an opportunity of pouring your love out to God, opening yourself completely to Him and when you confess in that way, then, of course, God forgives you through the priest. He pours His Holy Spirit out in abundance through the priest. So now in and through those two wonderful sacraments of reconciliation and of the priesthood, the loving forgiveness of God is poured out in a wonderful way which cleanses and heals your soul. Confession is more than forgiveness, which of course is the greatest part of it but it is also a healing sacrament.

For those who are sick: If you want true healing, you can find it through confession. When you come and truly open your heart to God and confess everything and allow God to purify your soul through the priest, as He removes the stain of sin from your soul, He removes the pain and the hurt that comes with it. Once your soul is healed, it is natural that other healing would follow.

Coming to confession for healing, it is important you do not let satan get hold of your pride so that you feel embarrassed about your sins and do not confess them. Sometimes people hold back the really bad sins and they do not tell the priest but they have forgotten that God knows everything about you, your bad thoughts, your bad actions and even when you are alone sinning, He is watching you.

Jesus explained to me "Understand, I have been with you every moment of your life! I know everything you have done. I know all the good things and all the bad things because I have been there, standing at your side. I know every breath you have taken, I know every word you have spoken, every thought you have had, every action you have done, I know.

"I know you inside out because I created you. I know you, I understand you, I have been there. Understand, when you were alone sinning, when no one else was there and no one else saw you – I did! I was next to you, watching you, crying for you, aching for you. Longing for you to understand the bad things you were doing but I love you so much that no matter what you have done, I will forgive you."

However, you must confess everything. Do not hold anything back. Understand, when you feel guilty, ashamed, embarrassed, understand this is satan getting hold of your pride, your weaknesses so that you will not confess.

When you do not confess, you hold on to those sins and then it is much easier for him to drag you deeper and deeper into sin, further away from God.

All God wants you to do is come and tell Him what He already knows. If you truly loved Him, you would do that automatically as in true love, there is no shame, there is no embarrassment. Of course, there is sorrow for your sins, but in love you know that God will forgive you everything.

True love of God draws you into the sacraments and brings them alive. In confession, now you start to see the depth of God's love. You realise Jesus died individually for you. He went through torment and gave His life and shed His blood for every one of you. So that no matter what sin you did, even the most grievous sin, He would forgive it if you come to Him in love and ask for that forgiveness. When you do that and allow Him to wash you with His precious blood and allow His Holy Spirit to cleanse and heal your soul, then in that moment in confession, your soul is purified.

In that moment until you sin again, your soul is perfect. Your soul is wide open, completely open to God, open to receive greater graces, greater gifts. There are no more barriers of the world and sin between you and God. Your soul is shining in His glory, waiting to be filled with His glory. Now in this pure state God, in His mercy, lifts you up into His divine grace and fills you with grace and strengthens your gifts. Now you are completely open to His grace which He pours inside you to strengthen you so that you can face and overcome sin in Him. In that moment when your soul is pure, God, if you allow Him, draws you into the mystery of His merciful love. In that pure moment, before you sin again, in that perfect state, God embraces you and in the depth of your soul, you feel the mercy of His forgiving love and the joy, the happiness that comes with that is beyond this world. Then you come to understand that confession is more than the merciful forgiveness of God, that confession is more than healing.

If in this moment you keep your focus on God and cry out your thanks for His forgiveness, for His love, desiring to embrace Him in this holy sacrament, then He takes the scales away from your eyes. He opens up the spiritual and the mystical to you as you now start to see and experience the sacrifice of Christ and the power of that sacrifice on the cross. You come to understand how God's love and mercy spans eternity as He draws you into the mystical forgiveness of the cross.

Clearly you see how all evil throughout eternity was defeated by His sacrifice on the cross and then you realise that all evil in your life is being defeated by His sacrifice when you embrace it. As you embrace the sacrifice of Christ in every moment, you embrace His love on the cross and you allow that love to pour out through you to bless the world through you and help in the defeat of evil.

Experiencing confession in this way makes it no longer a sacrament of which you think you should only do now and then. Now confession is no longer a difficulty, a burden. It is no longer something you avoid because you are ashamed of yourself. Now you have a burning desire to come to this sacrament and bow before your God and open your heart to Him, asking Him to strengthen you in your weaknesses, to forgive you for your sins, and the strength not to sin again.

It is obvious most Catholics do not see God's love and grace in confession because they come to confession so rarely and when they do, it is only to confess their sins maybe because of guilt. Not to open their heart and soul completely to God in love, calling out, "I'm sorry, Lord, that I have offended You, that I have hurt You. Forgive all of my sins. I have been so foolish, Lord. Forgive me and fill me with Your grace. Show me how to live."

Then when the Holy Spirit through the priest forgives your sins and the precious blood of Jesus washes over you to heal you and cleanse you, if you reach out to embrace that forgiveness believing the Holy Spirit is now purifying your soul you are open wide to His grace. As you reach out to God in that sacred moment, inside you is the knowledge that you will sin again so you beg God for the grace, you beg God for the strength to avoid sin for now you realise that sin is a barrier between you and God. It stops you loving Him completely, being completely open to Him.

In that pure moment, if you reach out to God in love, if you reach up to heaven, calling to God for His love, then He lifts you up to levels of grace you could have never imagined, to show you the wonder of His merciful and sacrificial love. In this pure state, until you sin again, your soul is ready and desiring to be filled with the grace of God. But you have to seek that, you have to want that by reaching out to God and saying, "God, fill me with whatever You want. Fill me with all I need to live my faith."

It is when you accept this grace from God, that He leads you along this path of perfection. He draws you into holiness in Him, along the path that walks upwards to heaven and the more you come to confession, the more you are led closer to heaven and filled with the grace that comes from God in heaven.

Now the gifts and graces that God has given you – because we are all gifted, we all are graced, – they grow and grow as you recognise who you truly are and you recognise the greatness of God's forgiving love and of His divine mercy and you live for that.

It is in confession when you focus on God and cry out your love for Him, that your heart and soul open wide and God pours His divine grace inside you to lift you up on the cross with Him to experience the mystery of His divine mercy. In that way your spirituality is strengthened as the mystical forgiveness of God is opened up for you. Every time you come to confession in this way God will show you a different aspect of His forgiveness if you keep your focus on Him in that pure moment.

Then, as the Holy Spirit pours into you through the priest, you feel His grace, His gifts filling you. You feel your whole being reverberating in the love of the Holy Spirit as you are graced in this pure state and drawn closer to God and prepared to receive God in the Eucharist in the way you should – the way of pure love. As the Holy Spirit pours grace in abundance into your soul, you are embracing His grace in humble love of God and as you do, the Holy Spirit opens you up to His gifts and graces in wonderful ways. He starts to show you your faith in ways that you never could have imagined.

No wonder confession is under such attack as it is so important for our faith. It is the forgiveness of our sins, it is the strengthening of our faith, it is being drawn up to higher levels of grace. If you ask the Holy Spirit in that moment of pureness to open your eyes to the truth of God, you will experience the depth of His eternal mercy, His eternal love. You will experience things you would have never thought possible. But it is all up to you and to your free will.

So many Catholics do not go to confession and they wonder why their faith is weak. It is weak because your pride keeps you from confessing to God, your pride stops you opening your heart to God in love and allowing Him to draw you up to Him. As you hold on to sin, you close your heart to God and you close your heart to the truth of our Catholic faith.

If you truly understood what was there for you in confession, you would go frequently. The sacrament of reconciliation is a wonderful blessing and a powerful gift of healing. A gift that reflects and is full of the sacrificial love of Christ, Our Lord, Who, when you have a true confession, reaches down from the cross to embrace you, saying, "I love you and I forgive you."

— *Love and the Eucharist*
Once your soul is cleansed in confession, the desire for the Eucharist becomes a thirst, a longing, a hunger, an ache, as now you know your soul, your entire being can never be satisfied until it is filled with God in union with Him. Your very being, your soul cries out to be fed by God. Your soul longs to be filled by God, to be made one with God. In that pure state when you have been forgiven, your soul is then prepared to receive God in His fullness and so you have to come to the Eucharist, your soul leads you there, it drives you there.

Now the scales fall away from your eyes – the scales of sin, the scales of self, the scales of the world. You see how much God loves you

that first He would forgive you, forgive you anything because He just loves you. He loves you as you are. With all your weaknesses, with all your faults, He still loves you.

Then you realise He loves you so much that He lowers Himself to invite us in the Eucharist to become one in Him. In that realisation when you come to the Eucharist, you come with that first commandment filling you – to love God with your whole heart, your soul, your body, your mind, your entire being – now you come with a desire to give yourself totally to God in the Eucharist. You come in imitation of Jesus, Who is love. Just as He gives Himself completely to us in love in the Eucharist, now we come and give ourselves completely to Him in love in the Eucharist.

You cannot help but do this for your soul drives you to be like this in the Eucharist. It drives you with the love of God, which sets fire to your soul and it drives you with the hunger to be filled with God. So now you come and say, "Here I am, Lord. I am Yours. I give You all of me – my mind, body, soul – it is Yours, Master, possess me completely. Use me in any way You want." Calling out from your very soul,

"Master"! Not saying "Master" because you have to but saying "Master" because you truly believe He is the master of love. It is then when you say that and mean that in love that you bow down humbly before the Lord in the way you should. Then you are totally exposed to God. There is nothing between you and Him. The world is pushed aside. It is just you and God, no barriers and as Jesus reaches out to embrace you completely in the Eucharist, you return that embrace. As He fills your entire being with Him, then you experience love to its fullest.

Your soul sings out in joy the praises of God, the love of God. When you say those words, "We lift our hearts to the Lord," no longer are they just words, but you feel those words, you truly mean those words, they are an expression of your love of God. You truly take your heart and offer it to Jesus and then, in that most holy moment when God and man unite, when Jesus lifts our humanity into His divinity, He lifts our weak human hearts into His divine heart. Our hearts melt into His, to become one in His. He absorbs them totally into Him, He envelopes our hearts into His divine love.

United in Him, we become part of the holy offering of the Mass. As Jesus offers Himself up as a sacrifice to the Father, He offers us up with Him by the power of the Holy Spirit. So we become part of the sacrifice of Jesus lifted up to the Father. In Jesus, we can become sacrificial offerings of love to the Father, so that in Him, we can be holy gifts to God.

— *Love and union with the Holy Trinity*
It is then, as we are lifted on high in Jesus, we are drawn into the experience of the mysterious love of the Holy Trinity, the fullness of the Holy Trinity and it is then that Jesus opens us to the full mystical truth of God. We feel the Father's love filling us, embracing us and comforting us, drawing us into eternal love. We feel the love of the Holy Spirit filling us in abundance with His gifts, with His graces, with His power, with His strength. We feel the Holy Spirit setting fire to our heart, to our soul, so that in every Eucharist, our faith truly comes alive and we find fullness of life. Now, one in Jesus, we enjoy and experience the eternal love of the Holy Trinity, the one true God who wants to lift us on high so that we can reside in eternal love with Him.

When we come to the Eucharist with that total giving of self, God allows us to experience a touch of heaven. He lifts us beyond this world and allows us to experience a touch of that eternal love in our souls. All because Jesus, in His divine love, lowers Himself to allow us to share in His divinity. This is something all the prophets in the Old Testament never experienced and would have longed and loved to experience.

In that moment as we are lifted to share in His divinity, all of heaven celebrates. The angels, the saints they sing with joy, thanking God in love that He would lift mankind so high. They sing the praises of God, the mercy of God, the love of God. Eternity resounds with that joyful sound, except, of course, where the evil angels are. They are crying out in anger because they cannot accept that Jesus would lower Himself to allow humans to share in His divinity, which lifts mankind above any of the angels. How sad it is that all of heaven knows the power of the Eucharist, all of hell knows the power of the Eucharist, but most on earth do not and because of this people deny themselves so much. God will only come into you as much as you allow Him. If you want to push Him away, if you want to deny Him, in free love, He allows you to do that freely but if you want to embrace Him, He overwhelms you with His love.

So many Catholics are too busy being focused on themselves and on the world, too busy seeking signs and wonders everywhere else instead of looking to Jesus in the Eucharist and allowing Him to lift them up to this wonderful glorious height in Him. Here is the great treasure that God offers you, but so many Catholics are looking for treasures in the world instead of treasures in heaven.

The evil angels encourage our blindness and are working so hard to stop people coming to Mass, to stop them living the Eucharist. They want to take us away from God in the Eucharist and to focus on ourselves, to focus on the world so that we will not be filled with the power of this divine love, this divine love which is Jesus Christ, Our Lord. The evil angels know that in this moment, as we are drawn into the divinity of God and lifted up into the glory of His eternal love, our humanity is glorified in His divinity, and this is something they cannot stand. They are terrified to see us be filled with the victory of Our

Lord, Jesus Christ, in the Eucharist. So they are doing their utmost to keep us away so that we will not embrace the victory of the cross in every Eucharist and carry that victorious cross with us wherever we go, unafraid. Evil knows that when a billion Catholics start to do that, then the light of Christ is going to shine so brightly in this world that darkness will flee and paradise will come to earth.

The evil angels also encourage the thoughts that Mass maybe is a little bit boring but Mass only becomes boring when you focus on the world. When you focus on heaven in the Eucharist, it is the most exciting, it is the most wonderful thing that God gives us for it is God giving Himself to us in love.

It is in that moment, as we are allowed to share in the divinity of Jesus, that heaven and earth unite. The Church is complete when we unite with Christ, because now the heavenly Church and the earthly Church become one in Christ. In that divine moment, when Jesus in love draws us into divine love, when He absorbs our weak human hearts into His divine heart. He lifts us on high, He lifts us beyond this world to experience His eternal and His mystical love and because of that your spiritual life becomes so strong. Now you desire only to live for God as you are meant to. Now in each moment, your very soul is content because that small touch of His love that you experienced in the Eucharist is greater than all the things of the world put together. You will find fullness of life on earth because you are filled with peace and love in each moment and in each moment you will feel the love of God surrounding you. Your soul, your spirit now dances in the joy of His wonderful grace.

As you receive Jesus in this way, you find the power to love. For as He draws you into His divine self and opens His heart completely to you, He pours out His never ending love into your heart to change your heart to become like His heart. Here in this divine moment you find the strength to love at all times, you find the strength to be like Jesus. In this holiest moment every person can be transformed to become the person he or she were created to be, a holy loving person who truly is an image of God. That is what we were created to be – an image of God, God Who is love. In the Eucharist, God, Jesus, helps us to become that image of God's love. As He lifts you up to mystical levels of love, you experience the fullness of God, the fullness of love, which is beyond the emotional, beyond the physical as it is the love of God in man.

You start to experience the sweetness of the spiritual and mystical love of Christ as He draws your mind, body and soul into His Body, Blood, Soul and Divinity. Drawing every cell of your being into Him, He then starts to change you in love, to mould your heart so that you become the person you are meant to be. He changes our very beings to be images of Him. It is Jesus in the Eucharist Who is changing lives, changing souls and changing the world. All it takes for this to happen to you is to come to Jesus in the Eucharist and truly say from your heart, "Here I am, Lord, I am Yours, truly make me Catholic."

It is then when you are drawn in this mystical way into Christ, Our Lord and allow His Body, Blood, Soul and Divinity to fill you completely, you find the strength to love because you have the strength of Jesus' eucharistic love within you. As you are drawn up to experience that love, you never want to lose it again because it lifts you beyond the world. The things of the world now become not so important for now you experience a touch of the eternal love of God in your heart and soul. Then you know what is waiting for you in heaven so now you cannot do anything else but live your life for God.

You realise your life on earth is only a moment in eternity, a blink of an eye. An important moment, where you can grow in the love of God and bring others to love God, but you realise that you must live for the life to come, knowing that is the greatest treasure of all. Now that you have had a taste of heaven in your very soul, this is all you desire. It is sad that most Catholics do not experience this, it is clear they do not because churches are so empty at times. If Catholics would experience unity with God as they are meant to in the Eucharist, the churches would be packed every day. As not only you, but others too, who would see the love of Christ in you, would be drawn to the Church.

Every Catholic is offered the opportunity to change, to truly be Christ-like because in every Eucharist, as you give yourself completely to Jesus, as He draws you into His divine being, He changes you to be the person you are meant to be – an image of God, God Who is love. You experience what is far beyond the world as Jesus lifts your heart into His heart and then in love as you let Him, He moulds your heart, to be an image of His Sacred Heart.

When He draws your heart into His heart, you realise that in His heart, He has a place for everyone, that He loves everyone. Then you realise if your heart is to be like Christ's, you, too, have to love everyone and you must serve everyone and thoughts of self disappear because now all you want to do is please God.

As you come and unite in humble love with Jesus in the Eucharist, when you cry out for His love, long for His love, live for His love, then as He draws you into His divinity and lifts you on high, He glorifies you in Him. In that eternal moment you can experience the eternal love of God, united in the love of God, united in God. He opens up the mystical and eternal realms to you so that you can experience that in every moment in the Eucharist.

This is what so many saints have experienced and God calls you to be saints. He calls you to experience this in the Eucharist if only you want it and truly desire it. When you come to the Holy Mass and truly look beyond self, when you give yourself totally to God, regardless of the cost, then you, too, will find holiness in the Eucharist.

Unfortunately most Catholics do not look for the spiritual and mystical in the sacraments, they are too busy looking to self. No wonder the churches are empty. If you truly experienced Christ in the Eucharist, you would be at Mass every day. You could not live without it because you would find fullness of life in Christ, Our Lord. When you start to live the Eucharist that way, then you start to understand what God has given us in this faith. The greatest gift of all, the greatest love of all, God Himself.

You come to understand why so many were prepared to give their lives for God for now, with God's love filling you in this complete way, you are prepared to give anything for Him. This is how your faith is meant to be. Sadly so many of us Catholics do not want to live that way, they are happy to sit back and let others do it. No wonder you see so little in your Church, in the sacraments and in your life because you are not living as you are supposed to.

Jesus said, "Unless you eat of My Body and drink of My Blood, you shall not have life within you." Today so many of us are dead in our faith because we are not living in the living God Who is present in the Eucharist, Who is the Eucharist.

When you begin to live the Eucharist, now in every moment you look to Jesus in love. As you look upon others, you remember how God loves them as He loves you and because you love God and because you allowed God to change you to be His image, you love everyone. You cannot help but love them. You cannot stop loving because your heart is beating in union with Christ's heart.

God loves the sinner. He loves the ones who killed Him. That's the depth of His love. He will forgive anyone anything and we are meant to do the same. He loves everyone regardless of what they have, regardless of who they are and what they look like. To God, they are all beautiful and they are meant to be beautiful to each one of us because in them, we should see the wonderful gift of God's love. It is when you start to live in love as you are meant to, you see the divine truth of humanity.

No longer are you a prisoner of the world. You are set free in Christ. All the money, all the things of the world, they mean little. They are like a grain of sand compared to the love of God because to experience God's love in this way is beyond the world. So you lose your desire to seek more and more. Now you want less and less in the world so that you can have more in God by giving yourself humbly to Him in love.

It is when you experience union with Christ in this way, truly you start to live your faith because now having tasted the sweetness of His love, you know it is worth living for, you know it is worth dying for, you know it is worth everything. When you experience this in the Eucharist then your worldly life comes into perspective. All that is important now is the eternal love of God and it is now in that love that your life on earth becomes complete.

No longer do you worry about what other people think about you. You are only concerned about what God thinks. No longer do you try and please the world or please yourself or please others, now you only want to please God. No longer can you live the way of the world, you only want to live the way of Christ. It is then that Christ lives in you in every moment for when you receive Him in this way, when you leave the church, you do not leave Christ behind; He leaves with you. You are living in Him and He is living in you. Every step you take He is taking with you. Every good word you say He is saying with you, every good action you do He is doing with you, every time you are reaching out to others, He is reaching out with you. Every heartbeat you are having He is having with you. Every thought you have He shares and every cross you carry, He carries with you.

As you go out to the world in this way, He pours out His grace, His love to touch others, to change their lives and to change the world. This is the faith that Christ, Our Lord gave us, the living faith, the loving faith, the faith we must live in the Eucharist through loving the Eucharist as it is here we find the love of God.

In the Eucharist you find fullness of life as now you are filled with the joy, the peace, the love, the excitement of God in each moment because now He is living in and with you as you are living in and with and through Him. Once you experience all this in the Eucharist, you will never want to be away from it because it is beyond anything of this world.

When you live in and with the Eucharist, never again are you a prisoner of the world, never again are you afraid of anything, never again are you miserable or unhappy. Now inside you, you are experiencing the eternal love of God and you start to become aware of what awaits you in heaven. The fear of death is taken from you because now you know in your heart, your soul, in your very being what is to come – love in eternity.

I hope and pray that all of you will come to the Eucharist with an ache, with a longing, with your heart and soul hurting for Jesus. Coming in that way and allowing Jesus to draw you into Himself, then in that eternal moment you can experience the love of heaven and you can experience the love of every person who has come in love to receive Jesus in the Eucharist. As from the Last Supper until the last Holy Mass, everyone who comes and receives Jesus in love becomes one in Him eternally and God offers you to experience this in every Eucharist if only you come and freely and totally love Him in the Eucharist.

The power of sacred priesthood

The other wonderful thing that happens as you now start to see in this spiritual way – you see priests in a different way. Just as I did when I first experienced this. In the Eucharist, the Lord started to show me the sacrament of the priesthood, one that I had never truly appreciated. It was one of the first times during Holy Mass, as I looked to the priest at the altar, he was shining completely white.

I saw that by the grace of God, in the Eucharist, the priest is filled completely with the Holy Spirit in a way no other person can be, far beyond anyone else. Regardless of the priest's weaknesses, he is lifted up to levels of grace that no one else can achieve – whether or not the priest understands this. When God lifts the priest to these high levels of grace, He fills him with holiness, with grace, with love, with power. Power that no one else can achieve. Then through the holy sacrament of the priesthood that grace is poured out through the priest, magnified through the priest to touch the people in the parish, the people all around, to draw them closer to God.

As I looked to the priest, I saw him change and he became Jesus before me and I realised in the Holy Mass, he truly is. In the Holy Mass, in every Holy Mass, there is Jesus in the priest. I realised that in every Holy Mass is the Last Supper. There is Jesus in the priest inviting us to the Last Supper, inviting us to be the apostles that join Him at the table. It is Jesus at the Last Supper, inviting each one of us to the table with Him so that we can be the apostles of today. I saw that when we partake of the Eucharist, that we become part of every Eucharist from the Last Supper to the last Holy Mass that is celebrated. How in Jesus, we unite with everyone else who received Him in love in the holy Eucharist, so that we all become one in Him and all by the grace that is poured out through the priest. All because Jesus, through the priesthood, invites us to come and eat of Him and drink of Him.

By the grace of the Holy Spirit, I now realised that in the sacred moment when bread and wine are changed to become Our Lord and God, Jesus Christ, the hands of the priest become the hands of Jesus at the Last Supper. The heart of the priest, even when the priest cannot understand this, becomes the heart of Jesus at the Last Supper.

The voice of the priest becomes the voice of Jesus during the Last Supper.

It became clear that the priest is filled completely with the power of heaven, with the power of God and I saw the priests had the most powerful hands in the world. Through their hands, by the grace of God, the bread and wine is changed into the Body, Blood, Soul and Divinity of Our Lord, God and Saviour, Jesus Christ. In this moment, the power of God, the power of heaven pours out through the hands of the priest. It is a power that is beyond the power of anyone else. A power that is greater than all evil. No wonder priests come under so much attack.

I saw how powerful the priesthood is, something I had never known before. In the Eucharist, I saw the power of the Holy Spirit filling the priest and coming out of the priest in each word. Each word, which is filled with the grace of the Holy Spirit, the power and the love of the Holy Spirit and I could feel that power touching me and lifting me beyond myself.

Looking at priests in life, I saw they truly imitated Jesus for by becoming a priest, they are offering their life totally to God as Jesus offered His life totally to the Father. These men, in love of God, give themselves totally to Him. They just love God and want to serve Him and in obedience to the second commandment, they just want to serve and love people and so willingly and freely they give their whole life for God and for you. A true example of following those two greatest commandments and how evil hates that! No wonder evil attacks the priests.

In their holy lives the priests carry many crosses and sacrifice so much in imitation of Christ and often they carry these crosses because we do not want to carry them ourselves. In their love of others, the priests and religious ask God to give them some of your crosses. In love, they willingly carry crosses for you and sometimes those crosses get so heavy that they fall down. Today many of us imitate the Jews at the time of Christ. At times we judge and condemn the priests, we expect them to do everything for us as many of the Jews expected Jesus to do what they wanted. Yet we expect to do so little for the priests. How selfish and how blind that is! It just shows we are looking with worldly eyes and not with heavenly eyes, because in every priest, regardless of their weaknesses, you should see Christ.

When Jesus fell down with His cross and struggled to get up, most did nothing to help. Only one brave woman stepped forward to help willingly while a man was dragged from the crowd to help and was blessed for that. We reflect those people because so few of us step forward to help the priests when they fall down. When you see a priest who falls down with heavy crosses, do not condemn or judge him, because when you do that, you are just like the Jews who condemned Jesus when He fell down. When you see a priest struggling, see Christ struggling with His cross and do not be the one to turn away but be the one to help Him carry the cross because the blessings for you will be great indeed.

Sadly today, so many of us do not help the priests carry their crosses, only a few step forward. We have been blinded so much by the world that we do not see that we are turning away from Christ when we behave in this way. Every time you see a priest, do not look upon their weaknesses and their mistakes, but look at their sacrifices.

— *Priests under attack*

It is so important that we help the priests. We should not condemn them, judge them or gossip about them. There is enough of that being done from people outside the Church. Why are we attacking our own Church? How satan laughs when we do that. We should be forgiving and loving our priests when they do things wrong because surely, when we do things wrong, we come to a priest and expect forgiveness and love. What a terrible double standard we have! Why can we not do the same to priests and show forgiveness, no matter what they have done? This is what we expect for ourselves.

Jesus forgives sinners. If He did not, He would not have come to earth, would He? He would have turned away from every one of us for we are all sinners. As Jesus forgave, we as Christians, we are meant to forgive. Yet so many of us do not, we condemn, we judge, we gossip. How satan laughs because now, we the people in the Church, weaken the Church ourselves. We are supposed to strengthen the Church by helping our priests, by praying and praying for them, by offering sacrifices for them. We should be defending the priests, defending the Church, and standing up and helping them if they do fall down.

If they do fall down, understand that reflects on us because they come from among us and so their weaknesses are reflections of our weaknesses. So we have to come and help the priests – not condemn, not judge – and in doing so, help those priests focus back on God, so they can look to heaven as they are meant to. Then their priesthood can be lifted up to those levels of grace to be brought to fullness in Christ, Our Lord, and as their priesthood is brought to fullness, they bring holiness into our lives. They lead us to holiness, they lead us to God and they lead us deep into the sacraments where we can find the same grace – not to the same levels – but we can be filled with grace to become the vessels of grace we are meant to be for the whole world.

Truly, priests are there to draw us into holiness but because priests have so much worldly work to do that they cannot focus on their saintly life. So often this is because we do not help them. If only we would help them more, they would have more time to focus on holiness. If they can do so, they will grow in holiness and will be filled with the light of the Holy Spirit, which will reach out through the priest to draw his parish, his flock, higher and higher into holiness.

When priests do the worldly things, their focus is in the world, not on God but if we can release them of these duties, we can help bring their focus back to God. If their focus is on the world, it is so easy for them to fall down like every one of us, because they are human, they are weak, just as we are. However, if we can take a lot of that away from them, and allow them to focus on their priestly ministry, on the sacraments, on prayer, on Holy Scripture, as they do that, God will draw them to holiness and lift them up to these high levels of grace. He will fill them with such gifts way beyond our understanding and then as they explode with His grace, it will pour out to touch all the people around and draw them closer to God.

So when you are helping priests, you are actually helping yourselves and this is what you are meant to do, you are the Body of Christ. We are the mystical Body of Christ on earth, and we are meant to work within the Church for it to grow, not to work to destroy it. Sadly today, so many people are quick to condemn priests, to judge priests. They look at the splinter in the priest's eye and the plank in their own eye is forgotten. How sad that is! Of course, when priests do things wrong, they must be held to account but they must be forgiven also.

The Lord Jesus once said to me, "Today, satan is so clever. What he does, is he stops people helping in the parishes. Less and less people are helping, offering their services, and the priest has to do more." He has to do things like counting money, and he has to do things he should not be doing, like cleaning the church. I have seen some priests doing that when we should be doing that! When the priests are doing that, they have less time for the sacraments, less time for Mass, less time to help the sick. This is what they should be doing because the priests' prime duty is to lead us in the worship of God, not to clean the church, not to count the money, not to be writing letters to the parishioners about parish activities. That's the things we should be doing! But today we are saying, "Let someone else do it. I'm too busy." Then we wonder, "Why is it that there is not so many confessions in church, why are there so few Masses? Why are there so few priests?" We look to the priests and blame them, and we forget it is our fault because we are shirking our responsibility.

Each one of us is part of the Church, part of the Body of Christ, and it is our duty, our responsibility to share in the work load, not to let the priests and nuns carry it all and then to blame them when things go wrong. Look to yourself and see what you are doing for God in His Church and what you are denying God in this Church and I am sure then you will see – there is much more you can do.

Do not turn away, step towards the priests, the Church, offer them your help, offer them your love. Then you will see, there will be more sacraments, there will be more Masses, there will be more people coming to church because the priest then will have more time to spread the faith, to evangelise. Today, they are burdened down so much. Jesus showed me a vision of Himself, surrounded with chains, weighed down in chains, and He said, "This is how the priests are today. Burdened by so much that others should be doing but are refusing to do."

Some Catholics also try to manipulate the priest to do what they want. Some Catholics try to make priests their servants. Priests are servants of God who in the love of God readily serve us, it is in that sacrificial offering of their lives, priests imitate Jesus in His sacrificial giving of His life. So instead of trying to manipulate priests and trying to get them do what you want, we are supposed to help priests and do what they ask of us. We are meant to respect them and the gift that Christ, Our Lord, gives us in them. Not to do so is not only insulting the priest but also insulting Christ. Today many people have forgotten what the priesthood is and they should start to remember. It is a great blessing from God. It is a blessing that should not be rejected, abused or treated badly, but it should be loved and respected.

It is very interesting sometimes I get some very devout Catholics who say to me, "I live the way of Christ, I never put the world first." Occasionally I ask them, "Do you ever talk to your sons, to your nephews, to your grandsons, to the young men around, about becoming priests?" Most say, no. Most encourage their young men to be doctors, lawyers, engineers, to be successful in the world, any thing but a priest. All of a sudden this world has become more important than the spiritual and mystical world and people see so little value in the priesthood but the priesthood has enormous value in eternity. However, because we are blinded by the world – even the devout – have forgotten this at times.

Obedience

The two greatest commandments, to love God with your whole heart, your whole mind, your whole body, your whole being and to love one another as Jesus loves us, these two commandments lead to everything else. They lead you deep into the sacraments and they lead you to an essential part of our faith that many have forgotten – obedience.

When you love God completely, giving your life totally to Him, loving Him above all others, above all else, above even yourself, you have a desire inside you to be obedient because this is an expression of your love of God. You do not want to hurt or offend the one you love, you want to please Him and one of the fruits of loving and pleasing God is obedience.

You are not forced to be obedient, you are willingly obedient to the commandments as you see the commandments in a new way. You see they are commandments of love given to help you stop destroying yourself, destroying your life and to help you live the right way. You realise it is not God demanding from you but it is God guiding you to do what is best. It is God saying to you, "I love you so much, I am giving you this guidance so you can find a full and happy life. I do not want you to suffer, I do not want you to be miserable, I want you to be happy."

All God says to us is, "I love you. Love Me, love one another, love and respect yourselves and live a good life." Yet that seems so difficult for many Catholics. To love God, to love each other, love your parents, not to lie, cheat, steal, do not be jealous, do not commit adultery … all the commandments are good things. They only become difficult when you start to close your heart to the love of God and you let the love of self and the love of the world reign in your heart.

— *Obedience to the Catholic Church*
It also becomes natural to be obedient to the Catholic Church as you realise this is the house of the Father, it is the Body of Christ, it is filled with the Holy Spirit. So how can you not be obedient to it? Now with the total acceptance of loving God before yourself, your eyes are opened to see the truth that when the Church speaks, it is the Holy Spirit speaking to you. You long to be obedient realising that the Church is telling you again only good things. Unfortunately many Catholics are drawn into disobedience, they forget who was the first to be disobedient to God. It was the prince of disobedience – Lucifer himself - and in disobedience that is the one we imitate. Yet, so many Catholics question, so many walk away from the Church because they disagree with things. Forgetting when we are disobedient to this Church, we are disobedient to God. In true love of God, you desire to be obedient. Your heart, your soul calls out to show your love in obedience to Him and to His Church.

No wonder so many Catholics are confused today because in love of self, in love of the world, they turn into disobedience and the confusion and unhappiness that comes with it. They make excuses to ignore some of the commandments and when they do that they are rejecting God and His love.

The saints remind me over and over that God gave us this Church. They said, "Living your faith means being obedient unless something goes against faith and morals." They explained, we should have a blind obedience because when we have that type of obedience, we are totally trusting in God, placing our hand in His and walking with Him and that is when we truly see. Today there are so many problems in the Church and people blame everyone else except themselves. They blame the priests, the nuns, the Church itself. Yet most of the problems in the Church come from disobedience. If only people would live an obedient faith, this Church would be strong, it would be vibrant and it would be full at every Mass. Sadly, due to pride, many Catholics do not live that way.

So many Catholics come to me with confusion in their lives and they say, "I do not know what God wants in my life, what can I do?" All that confusion shows me is a weakness of faith because if you had a strong faith, you would know that you have to do the same as the early Church did – you have to follow Christ without question, even if it means giving your life. In the early Church, whole families walked to their death because they loved God, they loved Christ and they wanted to be obedient to His will. How many of us are like that today? Most of us are disobedient, walking away from God and we wonder – we wonder why we suffer and why we have so many problems in our lives.

Understand that when you live in obedient love of God, He looks after you, He takes care of you, He brings peace, joy and happiness into your life! It is when you step away from God, when you step out of His love that evil is there to bring confusion, to bring hurt, to bring pain, to bring suffering. If you have problems in your life, first and foremost, look to God in His Church and live in His Church totally committed to obedience. When you do that, you will find, by the grace of God, your life will change. He will give you the strength you need to carry your crosses. He will change your life to bring joy, to bring happiness into your heart.

Yes, you may struggle and things may be hard, but always you know that God is with you, taking care of you, looking after you, protecting you. You know that in the end, heaven is your reward because that is the guarantee of being obedient to His Church, the guarantee that Jesus gave us. If we are obedient Catholics, heaven is ours.

Unfortunately many Catholics are looking to other ways to find heaven but it is the straight and narrow path, the path that Jesus walked, the path that is Jesus, that has to be followed. He walked obedient to the Father. We have to imitate that and walk the same path in obedience to the Body of Christ, the House of the Father that is filled by the Holy Spirit. Do not look anywhere else. You do not need to.

There are some Catholics who look back to the Old Testament and think how foolish the Jews were. They kept ignoring God, and then in the New Testament, they denied God, but most of us are no different than them. Christ has come to earth, God has come to earth, showing us how to live, and in our pride, in our self, just as the Jews did, we keep denying Him.

— *The obedience of the saints*

Many of us look to the saints and admire them and think how wonderful they are but often we do not try to imitate them, ignoring the fact that every saint was obedient to God. Yet how can we expect to be saints if we are not obedient?

Once, when saying the Hail Mary's, I saw I should turn to Our Blessed Mother, to ask for her help, for her intercession. I saw the words, "Holy Mary." The Lord said, "If you want to be holy, imitate Mary. She is a perfect example of humanity, My Blessed Mother, so holy. If you imitate her, look to her life, see how obedient to God she was and be the same, then you, too, can be holy."

The Lord also said, "If you want to find eternal love, if you want to find your way to heaven, live as Mary did. Totally in love with God, serving God in all things and in love bringing God to mankind. If you live her way, heaven is yours."

Mary shows every human that we are called to holiness. This is how we are supposed to be. She shows us that through our weaknesses, we can still be holy. Mary shows us that we can attain holiness in this life if we are totally obedient to God, if we reach out to God and say, "Only in You, Lord. Only by You, only for You and only with You." Seeking no glory for your self but everything for God. Mary shows us that the fruit of loving obedience is holiness so look to Mary and try to imitate her.

— *Obedience towards the bishop*

When Jesus began speaking and appearing to me, He said, "If truly you want to live the life I call you to then it must be an obedient one, obedient in Catholicism." Jesus asked me to see my archbishop and tell him what was happening and ask for his permission to do God's work. I thought my archbishop would not see me. I mean, who am I, I am just a man on the street but by the grace of God he did see me and I spent a long time talking to him. He gave me permission to speak and has continued to give me permission for fifteen years now.

Jesus told me when I went to the archbishop, "If he tells you to stop, you stop immediately without question." I made that promise to Jesus that I would. Jesus said, that is the obedience He calls for from all people. That when the Church speaks, we listen and we heed the call of the Church, we do not question it and we do not doubt it. When we question and doubt, then we are doubting Jesus Himself, we are questioning Jesus Himself.

Jesus explained to me, when I look to my archbishop, I should see Jesus before me and I should listen as if Jesus was speaking to me. I hear so many Catholics saying to me, " If Jesus was speaking and appearing to me, I would do everything He said!" Well, Jesus is alive, He is here in this Church, He is here in every Eucharist and He speaks to you through the hierarchy of the Church and through the priests.

Sadly, many are looking elsewhere for God, are not looking to where He is – in the Church He formed, in the Body of Christ that He gave to us. If you want to find God and find what is His will in your life, it is very simple. Look to the Church, follow the teachings of the Church, do what the Pope and the hierarchy says, and then you live the way God wants. It is the moment you do not do this that you are not living the way of God wants.

— The teachings of the Church

Often people ask me, "How can I show God I love Him?" The way to show your love of God is by obedience. Obedience to His commandments and to the teachings of the Church He gave us, that is the Catholic Church. Some people deny these teachings and they have problems in their lives and they wonder why. Every commandment God gives us and every teaching is there to help us lead a good and holy life in Him but when we do not live that way, that is when we open ourselves to evil and invite problems into our life.

So many people are selective in their obedience to the commandments. They say, "I like this one, I'll obey that one, but this one is too hard, let's ignore it." Also with the teachings of the Church there are so many who say, "Well, the rest of the world does not agree with that, so I will not either." Understand that in doing so, you are denying God and you are denying yourself His love in your life? With every bit of disobedience, you close your heart and soul more to God and you invite evil, you invite satan into your life, it is no wonder that you suffer!

When I was told I must be completely obedient to the Catholic Church, the Church of love, I used to find it exceptionally hard at times. Like many Catholics, I used to say, "I like this commandment, I will obey that one but I do not like this one, so I will ignore it." It was the same with the teachings of the Church, I would be selective with those. Jesus said to me, "Why are you like that? Look at what the Church says. Everything it says is goodness and love, encouraging people to come closer and closer to God. Showing people how to avoid what is wrong, what is sinful, so as to stop the evil one reaching into their lives and hurting them. Unfortunately a lot of people turn away from the teachings of the Church. No wonder they are confused in life. No wonder life is so difficult."

It is when you ignore the truth of God, then the deceit of evil will lead you into turmoil. The Lord, Jesus, said to me, "It is essential that you be obedient to the Church." It is a shame that many Catholics want to question everything and they want answers to everything and they want everything proven to them. What sort of faith is that? Faith is trusting in God, trusting in His commandments and in His teachings, even when you do not understand them. It is when you do that you open yourself to His divine grace in a special way, a way that brings joy and happiness into your heart and soul.

— *Democracy*

Sometimes I hear people say the Church should be a democracy. What a terrible pride that is! This is man saying his will should come before God's will. The Church of God, the Catholic Church, can never be a democracy and if ever it becomes that, then it becomes a Protestant Church. The call to every Catholic today is to be obedient. It is the same call Jesus gave to His disciples and to His apostles. I hope and pray that most Catholics today would be like the apostles and the disciples and listen and follow Jesus in obedience.

— *Listening to visionaries and mystics*

If you listen to people like me speaking, those who are claiming to hear or see Our Lord, Our Lady or the saints, first and foremost, check and see what they say and what they are writing is in line with Church teaching. If it is not, ignore it. Cast it aside because God will not contradict His own teachings. This is impossible. Look and see if they are obedient to the church. If they are not do not listen to them.

Yet, I see so many Catholics who are reading things that are so far away from Church teaching and are being led into disobedience. No wonder they are confused! First and foremost, follow the Catholic Church. Understand anything God gives to someone like me will be to complement and strengthen your faith and strengthen your obedience to this Church.

The call for perfection

Trying to walk in the love of God every day, I came to realise this life on earth is only a moment in eternity. While it is a special moment where we can grow in grace and come to love God more and more so that we can live with Him eternally in heaven – it is only a moment.

When you realise that, no longer are you a prisoner of the world, no longer are you drawn into the imperfection of the world. Now you try and be perfect in all things for God for when you come to love God, you just want to please Him.

Jesus told us in Holy Scripture that we are called to perfection. Our Blessed Mother said to me once that I should live a perfect life. I said, "That is impossible! Maybe the pope or bishops or priests or nuns, or some of you good people here today, but not me."

She said, "You must try, that is the important thing. Yes, you will never achieve perfection on earth, that is impossible, because Christ is the only perfect One, (and of course His Blessed Mother who was pure by the grace of God) but you must do your best. You must try and be perfect in all things."

To be perfect means to love because love, true love, is perfection itself and you must avoid sin at all cost as sin draws you into imperfection. Sin is a cancer that eats away at your soul and draws you deeper and deeper into the dark. Like a cancer, it starts with a small sin, then the sins become bigger and bigger. Then you are sinning so much and accepting the wrongs of the world, and you are so far away from God that you do not understand how you got there and how you are being drawn deeper and deeper into the dark.

Our Blessed Mother said, "That is why it is so important you must make every effort to stop even the smallest sin, a bad thought, a bad word about someone. Every time you start to think that way, turn you thoughts to perfection – to Jesus, Who is perfection." So every time I get a bad thought now, and believe me, I get many, as soon as I get them I start to think over and over in my mind, "Jesus, I love You." Then these bad thoughts just fall away and my focus is brought on Jesus, Our Lord.

Doing this instead of thinking of people badly, you can only think of them in love. Because you realise that Jesus loves them as He loves you and that Jesus loves even the worst sinner. Jesus loves those who irritate you, who annoy you and now you start to look with the eyes of Jesus as you realise, you must love them, too. It is love that brings us to perfection. God is love and God is perfect. He created us in His image, an image that is meant to be perfect.

The world and evil draw us away from God, draw us into immorality, into greed, into selfishness, into sin. Every sin, no matter what it is, is a denial of love, a denial of God and it stops you being lifted up to reach that perfection that you are called to.

The following are excerpts, mainly taken from a talk given at a Eucharistic Conference in the United States.

— *The meaning of life*
So many people wonder, "What is the meaning of life?" No Catholic should wonder that. Every Catholic should *know* that in the Eucharist the meaning of life is found and that is to love God and in the love of God to love others and in His divine love, to live joyfully eternally. This is our Catholic faith, a faith that so many Catholics deny because they are looking to the world rather than looking to heaven.

— *How to come to the Eucharist*
It is so obvious that most Catholics do not come to the Mass in true love of God because so many look as if they are bored in Mass, talking to their friends, thinking about self and wondering when the Mass will finish. All because they are experiencing so little in the Mass while you should be experiencing so much.

To celebrate Mass properly, from the first word till the last word you have to be focusing on the Father and the Son and the Holy Spirit calling out to God that you love Him, that you want His love. Aching for that love, longing for that love, thirsting for that love and anticipating with an excited heart, with a heart beating full of love for God, waiting and waiting to receive Him until that divine moment of bliss when you do finally receive Our Lord within in communion.

At every Mass, the first thing you should do when you come to the Eucharist is turn to the Holy Spirit and say, "Lord help me to celebrate this Mass in the way I should. Help me not only to receive Jesus in the way I should, the way of love, but help me to give myself completely to Jesus without reserve, without holding back." When you say that and mean that, then by the grace of God, you can come in imitation of Jesus, who gives himself completely to you and truly give yourself to Him.

It is when you come to the Eucharist in this way that you bow down humbly before God are putting the world and self aside so there are no more barriers between yourself and God, you are totally exposed to Him. He then reaches out and draws you into the Eucharist.

As you look to the priest at the altar, now you see he is completely full of the Holy Spirit in the Holy Mass, filled with grace in a way no other person can be. In the Holy Eucharist the priest is lifted to levels of grace that no other person can reach. As he is filled with this grace, it is poured out, it is magnified through him, to touch the people in the parish, to draw them closer to God. As that happens, every word of the Mass comes alive because now you become part of those words, you are drawn into them.

You see what the Holy Spirit is doing in the words that are leading up to communion. He is bringing your focus to God, away from self, so that you can receive Jesus in the way you are meant to, receive Him in love.

As you look at the priest then you see in the priest Jesus Himself. You realise it is Jesus at the altar inviting you to be one with Him in the holy sacrifice. Then as you come and receive Jesus in communion, in that most holy moment, in that most sacred moment, when God in humble love lowers Himself to come into us, in that moment when God and man unite, Jesus lifts up your humanity into His divinity. It is in that moment He allows us to share in His divinity and if you truly understood the greatness of this gift, every Mass and every church would be packed. If you just thought about that one thing, you could spend the rest of your life thinking on that and still not understand the greatness of that gift, the greatest of all gifts.

As you receive Jesus within, you realise that He is receiving you within as well and that now you are totally one with God, filled with His power, His love, His graces, His gifts. Now you start to see life in a different way, the way of Christ, the Christian way, for now Christ inside of you is changing you to be more like Him. As Christ takes you into Him, He changes you to be more like Him. That is what you are meant to be, like Christ – you are meant to be Christ to the world - but you can only truly be that if you give yourself totally to Him and accept Him totally within.

If people realised the importance of the Eucharist, they would be at the Eucharist every day. If you truly understood what Jesus offers us and understood what you received in sharing in His divinity, you would not be able to keep away from the Mass. It is as He draws us into His divinity and lifts us on high in Him that He opens up His eternal glory to us and glorifies us in Him. In that moment, if we have totally given ourselves to God, then we can experience His eternal and His divine love. Once you taste the sweetness of that, the world can never trap you again. Now you are free in God because you know that all the things of the world are like a grain of sand compared to what God gives you in the Eucharist.

— *Distractions and doubts during Holy Mass*
So many of us, even the devout, are easily distracted during Mass, and Jesus told me, "You are letting satan get hold of you. He knows your weaknesses. He knows what will distract you and he distracts you because he knows it is so important that you be completely focused on and open to God." If he can stop you accepting the Lord within you properly at any time, he will. When you think of self, when you are distracted you put up a barrier and you block the Lord's love from filling you.

Then we wonder why Mass becomes tedious at times. We wonder why it is a struggle. We wonder why it is easy to be distracted. It is because we are trapped in self and not looking to God. Now God, by His wonderful grace, helps me to overcome this, and by His wonderful grace He will help every one of you too. If, when you first come to the Mass, you turn to the Holy Spirit and say, "Lord, I'm weak, I'm fragile, I will be distracted. I trip up so easily. I look away from You so easily because I do not have the strength to look at You. But Lord, free me from my weakness, lead me, guide me to You. Pour out that grace. Keep me longing for You. Keep me aching and wanting You."

When you turn to the Holy Spirit and you say that and truly mean that, then the Holy Spirit pours His grace out deep inside of you. That grace will bring your focus back onto God, to where it is meant to be and then when you are focusing on God, by the grace of the Holy Spirit, that is when you start to celebrate the Mass properly. That is when it starts to come alive for every person. That is when it becomes full for you, full of love and of happiness, as it is meant to be. When that barrier of self fell away from me, the joy, the ecstasy I felt in the Mass just increased and increased. I saw that treasure that we have in each Mass, where God lowers Himself to come into us to fill us so we can be complete in love, complete in Him.

The greatest gift we have is the Eucharist, but so many people do not understand this or cannot believe it. I never did. I thought, "How can bread and wine be Jesus? How can it, it is bread and wine!" What I had forgotten is, God can do anything. He has created the universe, He has created you and me, and if He wants to change the bread and wine into His Body and Blood, He has got the power to do it and He does!

When the priest raises the Host above his head, often I see the Host bleeding with Jesus' face in it or a crown of thorns. Sometimes when I look at the priest, he becomes Jesus. The Lord explained to me, "The reason you are seeing this is because the priest is My image before you. He is My servant, he is standing in for Me to bring Me and My love to you and to bring you to Me." That is the priest's job to bring every person closer to God, to lead us in the worship of God. That is what priests are for.

When I received Jesus in the Eucharist and He lifted me into His Sacred Heart, I knew then, I could never be away from Him again. I knew that nothing in this world compared to the sweet love that is Jesus in the Eucharist and I had to be with Him every day. A lot of Catholics go to the Eucharist once a week or maybe once a month. Sometimes they go twice a week or three times a week and feel like they are doing something special. However, if you love your husband or your wife or your children or your family, you want to be with them as much as you can, you want to be with them every day. So why is it that when we profess to love Jesus, that once a week is enough or twice a week is enough? If you truly love Him, you want to be with Him every day. You want to be filled with His love, embraced with His love and lifted in His love every day. It seems many Catholics do not want that and then they wonder why they struggle in their faith, they wonder why their faith is weak. When your soul hungers, when your soul aches for God and you do not satisfy that hunger, satisfy that ache, that is when the confusion comes in. That is when you become uncertain, filled with doubts. That is when you get easily led away from God. But if you keep your soul satisfied in that divine love, that is Jesus Christ, Our Lord, then you are never uncertain. Doubts are overcome so easily because God gives you the grace, He gives you the strength to overcome them. All it takes is for you to come and satisfy your soul in that divine banquet which is the Body, Blood, the Soul and Divinity of Our Lord and Our Saviour, Jesus Christ.

— *Learning to love through the Eucharist*
I asked Jesus, "How can I love like You, how can I love like this? Your love is so overwhelming, it is so powerful. It is impossible for me, a mere human being, to love like You, Our divine Lord." Jesus replied, "Come to Me in the Eucharist. Lean on Me in the Eucharist. Find your strength in Me in the Eucharist. But when you come to the Eucharist, you must come not only to receive Me which, of course, is the greatest thing but you must come also and give yourself to Me." It is in that giving of self to Christ, Our Lord, that you push your pride, yourself aside and you open yourself totally wide to Him.

In every Eucharist, you should see the life, the death and the resurrection of Our Lord, God and Saviour, for truly, it is there. When you come to the Eucharist, you should say, "Lord, let me die to myself and be resurrected in You and find full life in You in this Eucharist. Possess me completely, my mind, my body, my soul, I give it all to You, use me in whatever way You want."

As you look with spiritual sight, you can come to see the death and resurrection of Our Lord, Jesus in every Eucharist. Now you long

145

to join with Him in that death, in that resurrection, so that you can find complete, full and true life in Him. However, this may only happen if you come and say, "Lord, let me die to self. Change me, use me. I have come to do whatever You ask of me." If you persevere and pray this in each Mass, then little by little, Jesus will help you to die to your self and come to life in Him. It is when you say that and mean that, in true love, you bow down humbly before Him, you take all your barriers away and now you are totally exposed to Our divine Lord and Saviour. There is nothing between you and Him.

As you are opened in this way of love to God, He comes inside you, totally filling you with His Body, His Blood, His Soul, His Divinity, strengthening every part of your being and changing you to be more like Him. That is what the Eucharist is meant to be, an experience of change where you become more and more like Jesus. To be like Jesus, you have to come to the Eucharist and ask Him to help you be like Him. You have to desire that, you have to want that, you have to ache for that. You can only become more like Him if you want to, if you want to put yourself aside, put the world aside and allow Jesus to embrace you completely in His divine Self.

Today, many Catholics do not have these desires. No wonder the sacrament of the Mass is so empty for many. No wonder that your lives are so empty because you do not live completely in Jesus as you are meant to and your soul inside hungers for Him, it cries out for Him, and so often, we ignore that.

Our God is the living God. He is alive in every Eucharist, and when we receive Him within, we are meant to come to life in Him, to live every moment in Him. It is when you come to the Eucharist in this way and experience this change, then in every day you will find the strength to love because now your human love is united with God's divine love. As you reach out in love to others, God reaches out through you, and with you, with His divine love. Then as you reach out to others, there is Jesus, reaching out with you and now when others see you, they see Christ in you. Just as they are meant to.

As a Christian, we are meant to imitate Christ, we are meant to be like Christ. We are meant to be Christ to the world but this is only possible if you live in Christ, our living God who is in the

Eucharist. It is by coming and dying to self in every Eucharist, that you can truly live in Him, totally free in His love, free and unafraid to share His love with everyone. This is the Catholic faith! The faith of love. The faith of divine and human love, the faith that sadly, so many do not live.

— *Healing in the Eucharist*

The Lord explained to me that the Eucharist is the greatest healing prayer of all and I find it very sad that many people today when they are sick, they go anywhere else except come to Jesus in the Eucharist.

This is where the greatest physician, God Himself, will heal you, heal you in the way that is best for you, physically, spiritually, emotionally. But you have to come seeking that healing, wanting that healing and believing in that healing. However, because so many Catholics do not even think about healing in the Eucharist they deny themselves so much.

In every Eucharist we say, "Only say the word, Lord, and I shall be healed." Well, in every Eucharist Jesus is calling out to each one of you, "Be healed!" Unfortunately so many of you are deaf, you are not listening. Open your hearts to God in the Eucharist and be healed! He gives you the best healing of all. He heals your soul, your mind, your body, your entire being. If you just give yourself to Him in total belief, no doubts, no fears, no concerns, just trusting in Jesus – Jesus, I trust in you. In the Eucharist is everything you need in this life for there is God Himself. What a sorrow it is that many of us are unaware of that, many of us are blind to that, many of us only say the words in the Mass but do not truly believe them or live them. We must live our faith, our Eucharistic faith.

The Lord explained to me, "In every Eucharist, I am there waiting for you to come to Me so that I can fill you with love, with joy, with happiness, with contentment." He said, "I want to lift all your suffering, all your pain, all your loneliness and you will find I do that in the Eucharist if you truly open your heart to Me, truly celebrate the Eucharist." He said, today many people are casual observers when they come to Mass. They come in, sit down, think about their families, their friends, their jobs, their school. Getting a bit bored if the priest goes on a little with his homily, looking at their watch, thinking when is this going to end? They are focusing on self, not on God.

The Lord said, "When you come to the Eucharist, when you come and spend that time with Me, focus on the Father and the Son and the Holy Spirit. When you come to the Eucharist, you must celebrate it truly. To do that, you must be part of every word that the priest speaks, every prayer you must join in and open your heart to God, reach out to God and say, "Lord I love You. I long for Your love, I want Your love, fill me with Your graces, gifts and the healing You have for me." Then God does it. He reaches out to overwhelm you when you do that and He gives you love, joy, happiness. He heals your lives, He heals your families. He offers you everything in the Eucharist, but it is up to you to come to Him and ask Him for, to beg Him for what you need. Accepting whatever healing God gives you as the best healing for you. Understanding there is God, divinity Himself, reaching out to you, allowing you to unite with Him, to become one with Him so you can be healed in Him in the way that He sees as best for you.

— *The kingdom of God*

When you come to the Eucharist, you should be seeking the kingdom of God. So many Catholics ask me, "Where is the kingdom of God? Where can I find Jesus?" You can find Him in every Eucharist, He is there reaching out to each one of you to change you and make you the people you are meant to be.

When a billion Catholics start to live their Eucharistic faith, and in the Eucharist come to live the death and resurrection of Jesus, the victory of Jesus, live that every moment in their life, then darkness will flee and paradise will come to earth. The kingdom of God will be here but you first you have to seek that in every Eucharist. Remember our faith is the victory of God and if we live that victory, then in us is the defeat of evil.

— *In the Eucharist love comes alive*

That is our faith – God is love and God is alive here in this church in the Eucharist, alive in love. That is what we are meant to live in – love but most of us do not and we still think we are living our faith. A faith without love is no faith at all. How sad that so many of us are blind to the way we are living and blind to Christ in our life – Christ who wants to bring us to true life in Him in every Eucharist.

For God to be able to fill us with His love, with His truth, with His gifts in the Eucharist, we have to invite Him completely within. Jesus will not force Himself upon us. He will only come in as much as we invite Him in. He gives us the free will to invite Him or not to and it is so obvious that many people do not totally invite Jesus in the Eucharist. It is so obvious that many think of self and think of the world when they come to the Mass, as when they receive Jesus in communion, they do not experience the fullness of His love. For this to happen, you have to pray every word of the Eucharist from your heart, from your soul, aching and longing for the love of God. When you invite Him within completely, He comes in His fullness to you and fills your entire being, every cell of you.

Every Eucharist is or should be a mystical experience for each person but for most it is not as we are trapped in the world and trapped in self. When we come to the Eucharist we do not have this spiritual sight to see. When you come to the Eucharist, you are meant to ask the Holy Spirit to open your eyes so that you can see the truth. When you do that *and you keep doing that*, then one day, it opens up for you and you see the truth of Jesus in every Eucharist.

The Eucharist is full of mystery, is full of wonders, is full of signs, is full of excitement, is full of love and is full of God waiting to fill you.

— *Different languages in Mass*

The Eucharist is now coming alive for me. I have to go every day. As the priest says the Mass, this powerful love keeps filling me. The words truly are fire, the fire of love and I want to taste them in every Eucharist.

I started going to different Masses. I went to Latin Mass, I have been to Aramaic Masses, Ukrainian rite, all sorts of Masses, in different rites and languages, French, German, Italian … Some people were saying to me, "Oh, it is only the Latin Mass that is truly the proper Mass. We should all have Mass in Latin." How foolish that is, how blind that is! It is not the language that makes the Mass holy. It is the Mass, the Holy Eucharist, when it is performed in the proper order, making the words holy! It does not matter in which language it is, each of those words is holy, is sacred, filled with the divine power of the Holy Spirit, the love of Jesus, and the grace of the Father – regardless of the language.

We have to be very careful because evil works on our pride to trip us up, to make us angry, to make us frustrated, because we maybe want the Latin Mass or Mass in a certain language. Understand, every language, by the grace of God, is holy in the Mass and appreciate each one. I go to Mass at many different rites within the Catholic Church and they are all wonderful.

This talk was given in October 2001 in the USA, just a few weeks after the terrorist attack on the World Trade Centre in New York.

Jesus Christ, Our Lord, is the Lord of love and forgiveness, the Lord of mercy. Sadly today, many Catholics, many Christians are not that way and when you are not that way, you are not Christ-like.

One of the things the saints told me was that I had to love God above all others, above all else, above even myself. As I started to pray on that and think on that, with their encouragement, it seemed so natural that I should do this. I realised that God had created everything, everyone, He had created me in His love and in all around me God's love was everywhere. I realised I existed and lived in His love. I realised that God must be a God of love who truly cares for me. If He loved me so much, then surely I should respond and give Him my total love and giving my total love to God will mean that I loved everyone else. How could I hate anyone or feel angry with them, because they are God's creation of love.

As I looked around, I began to admire the trees, the plants, the animals, the sun, the moon. I started to love everything. I saw everything was a gift of God's love to me and to everyone. It seemed so natural that if I tried to love God above all others, my life would become one of love with no hatred, with no anger, with no resentment. That if I truly loved God, also it would be natural to be obedient to Him because when you love someone, you want to please them. I found that as I loved God more and more, all I wanted to do is please Him in every moment of my life, to make Him happy in my life and when I started to do things wrong, I felt so sad and so disappointed with myself. Yet, the saints began to encourage me to look beyond this and keep reaching out to love God more and more.

When I started to do that, then in each person He showed me an image of Himself even in the terrorist who would kill me. The Lord explained "Here is an image of Me, show them love. Pray for them, reach out to them so that they can find My divine truth, My divine love in their life." That is what you are meant to do. However, especially in these times, it is so easy for Christians, for Catholics to be angry, to be bitter, to want this revenge. Yet that is not the way of Christ, surely that is not the way of God. God Who is love calls us to love. Calls us to live in His divine love, to be images of that love, to take that love to the world, but to do it by His power, by His grace, by His love, by Him in the Eucharist – and not by ourselves.

It is when we try to do these things by ourselves without God, that we are bound to fail, we are bound to fall down. As we fall down and as we stop loving, every time we stop loving, every time we start to hate, every time we start to feel bitter, every time we resent someone or any time we turn away from the prostitute, the drug addict, the murderer, the people in need, the sick, the people with AIDS – any time we turn away from them, we are turning away from Christ.

As we turn away from Christ, we turn into the dark where satan is waiting to take hold of us and lead us further and further away from God. Lead us to become self-centred, become greedy, not thinking of others, not thinking much of God and just living in our own little world and trying to change God to suit us. That is what many Catholics do today.

How sad it is today that many Christians do not live up to God's call of love. Recently we have had a very clear example of that with this terrible tragedy of the planes being crashed into the twin towers and killing so many. What a terrible sin, a terrible crime!

Yet so many Catholics are quick to condemn and to judge but we have no right to do that. I hear many Catholics say, "We have to attack other countries and kill people." We have no right to do that! We have to respond in love, for God is love and if we call ourselves people who love God, then we must be the same, not people who seek revenge. However it seems we are not. Sadly today, we have this big plank in our eye that stops us seeing how we are and yet we can criticise others so easily.

— *The roots of terrorism*

One of the things the Lord showed me this week with this terrible tragedy is that it should be a sign for change in people's lives. For truly we need to change to stop these things happening. I have heard so many Catholics blaming these attacks and disasters happening because of abortion, because of the death penalty, because of so many other things, and of course, all that evil contributed to that because it opens up this country (the USA) to more and more evil.

Yet, why is it that few look at the way they live? Most blame it on everyone else and are not looking to themselves.

The Lord told me, this must be a sign for each one of us to change. One of the reasons this bad thing happened was because Americans and Australians and English people, people in the West, who live in so much affluence, live with so much wealth, treat the people in the Second and Third World as less than them. When they see people starving, they really do not take much notice. When they see people in the Middle East being killed, "Well, they are only Arabs, their life is not as important as ours, it does not mean so much ..." All of a sudden, we are looking upon others as less than ourselves and placing more importance on ourselves and that is not the way God calls us to be.

God loves every person in this world equally. As Christians, as followers of Christ, Our Lord, as followers of God, we must be the same. But many are not. Many are quick to condemn those in the Middle East and when the people there get killed, their lives are so unimportant. Understand that is what breeds the hatred that causes those people to want to hurt you?

When I left England and I first started travelling around the world, I thought everyone loved English people. It is not true! A lot of people dislike English people throughout the world. I thought everyone liked Americans. It is not true! Many people dislike Americans. The reason they do not like the English and the Americans is that we have so much and often we have taken it through exploiting them. Also when they have so little, we do nothing to help them or very little. We give twenty dollars in a collection to ease our conscience and feel really good because we have given a little. We let these people suffer, die and starve. They get oppressed and get killed and we do nothing.

How many of you have stood up and complained to your government about the bad treatment of the people in the Middle East – families getting killed, children being killed. There is a deafening silence from Catholics. No wonder these people feel hatred towards us. No wonder they feel resentment. When we treat them as less than us, then we sow the seed of terrorism in this world.

— *Forgiveness is the source of peace*

I see so many Catholics today condemning the Muslims. So many are happy that the bombings are happening in Iraq and the revenge is happening. Many say, "An eye for an eye and a tooth for a tooth." Understand that is living to the Old Testament. In Christ, Our Lord, we are called to live the New Testament, the New Covenant, to be Christ-like.

Jesus is the fulfilment of the Old Testament and so we must live the New Testament. Jesus told us it is not an eye for an eye, it is not a tooth for a tooth – you turn the other cheek, you love your enemies! That is what we must live to. When you start to go and live to the Old Testament, then you are living more a Protestant faith and more a Jewish faith than a Catholic faith, the true faith that Jesus gave us. So live the way Jesus shows. Walk in His steps, the steps of love, the steps of forgiveness and you will find in your life peace will come upon you in such a way that you wonder why you never walked that way before.

Jesus said to forgive your enemy. For some it is the hardest thing to do but you must do it. If you want to be Christ-like, from the first moment someone hurts you, someone offends you, you must forgive them. It must be a normal response within you, because if it is not, then truly you are not imitating Christ. To have that way of forgiveness, that forgiving love, is only possible when you come to the

Eucharist, submit yourself totally to Jesus and ask Him by the power of His Holy Spirit to change you and to make you just like Him.

Jesus Christ, Our Lord, showed us in His life that we must love everyone and we must forgive everyone. Yet many Catholics are saying we should bomb these countries. The moment you think that way, the moment that is on your heart, then you are living away from God and you are opening yourself up to evil, up to satan who is waiting just to take you closer and closer to him.

If you have any hatred, you must pray to the Holy Spirit to take it from you. If you are having feelings of wanting anyone killed, you must pray to the Holy Spirit to take that from you. If you do not feel forgiveness in your heart for those people who committed these terrible crimes, pray to the Holy Spirit that you can forgive them. As a Catholic, your first thoughts must be of forgiveness and of love as that is the way of Jesus. When they killed Him, He had the power of heaven at His hands but He did not respond by destroying them. He went to the cross in love and with His last words, He said He forgave us and asked for forgiveness from the Father. As Catholics, as Christians, we must be the same. Our first words and our last words must be ones of love and of forgiveness and if they are not, we are not living a Christian life and we are Christian in name only.

— *Disasters can be a wake-up call*
So many Catholics complain about the troubles in the world, about all the bad things that are happening. They complain about the weakness in the Church, about all the problems we are having and the churches being empty. They look everywhere else and blame everyone else but do you look to yourself and see what you are doing? Do you look to yourself and in every Eucharist say, "Jesus, change me, change me to be how You want me to be."

Today, after that terrible tragedy a few weeks ago in the twin towers, there is so much condemnation, so much anger, so much frustration and so much hatred. That is not the way of Christ. Christ called us to forgive, to reach out in love, in kindness, in understanding. Those disasters should be a wake-up call for every Catholic. The call should be to each one of you, "Are you living your faith?" When we say yes to abortion, yes to divorce, yes to the death penalty, yes to homosexuality and many other bad things we draw evil to us. It seems the greater evil is, the more indifferent we are in our faith. How many of us are not living our faith and we think we are! So many of us come to church and we come to the sacraments, we pray, we read Holy Scripture, but as soon as we leave the church, we forget about God. We just talk about God in church or when we are amongst the people who know and love God but anywhere else, we are afraid to speak of Him, embarrassed to speak of Him and embarrassed to live our faith. No wonder the world suffers! It suffers because we are weak when we should be strong in our faith.

Understand that satan fears you if you live your faith and that our faith is a guarantee of heaven, our faith is a guarantee of victory. When we only live within the church in Christ, Our Lord, and do not take Him out to the world as Jesus commanded us to, then we are not living as God calls us to. Every one of you and every Catholic, when you leave a Mass, you should be going out of the church door and you should be taking the peace and the love of Christ with you. The priest says in the Mass, "The peace of Christ be with you." Yet, how many of you leave, full of concern, so anxious, so worried, no peace in your heart? His peace should be residing there so you can take that peace to others but sadly some are filled with anger, with frustration, with resentment, seeking revenge. Christ is never that way and we are not to be that way.

In every Eucharist, we are called to be like Our Blessed Mother. When she had Jesus within her, she went to Elisabeth who was in need and Jesus reach out from inside her to touch Elisabeth and John the Baptist within her and filled them with the Holy Spirit. Now you, too, can be exactly the same as Our Blessed Mother. When you are filled with Jesus in the Eucharist, if you say your fiat, your yes to living the faith and taking our living God and your living faith out the church door to everyone unafraid, then Jesus will reach out through you to touch others. But first it begins with you changing yourself, taking away the fear and just trusting completely in Our divine and eucharistic Lord. When you do that, then in your life the victory of Christ will be seen and through you that victory will reach out to many others.

— *Disrespect breeds hatred*

Often we do not look to ourselves correctly and we have that big plank in our eyes as we see the splinter in everyone else. First look to yourself and understand that in the West, we need to change. Responding with bombing and killing people is not going to stop terrorism. That is just a bad approach. We have to change our whole attitude towards the Third World, towards the Muslim world. As long as we are taking advantage of them, as long as we are exploiting them, as long as we are seeing them as less than others, as less than us, as long as we are seeing an Arab die in Jerusalem and think nothing of it. Seeing a child shot by the soldiers and thinking nothing of it because, "He is an Arab, he is a Palestinian, he is a terrorist." As long as we live this way, these problems are going to continue.

Jesus, Our Lord, loves every person on this planet, and if you call yourself a Christian, you must be the same. We must love the Jew, Muslim, Christian, terrorist, whomever, equally, because Christ, Our Lord, does. We must reach out in His love and in our faith, which is the true faith, to those people and treat them with respect, with kindness, with love. Not taking advantage of them, not rejecting them, not turning away from them and not seeing them with eyes of contempt. It is when you do not do that, you breed hatred and do not solve the problem of terrorism but help it grow. This hatred is out there because we are exploiting the world and we should not be. Every Catholic and every Christian should be standing up and saying, "This is wrong! Our governments need to change, we need to treat every person with respect."

So many people here in the U.S.A. are talking about the right of life of the unborn babies that are terribly destroyed in abortion. Of course, we should speak up against abortion, this terrible sin which is the most horrible sin and should be opposed by all Christians if they are to be truly Christian. Sadly, some Catholics, some Christians vote for pro-abortion candidates and see no wrong in that. Well to do so is a grave wrong and places the one who does so in a state of grave sin regardless of what excuse they used to vote for that person. But why is there not the same cry about the people in the Third World that are being killed? While there are less being killed than the poor babies this is still a serious wrong while not of the same gravity as the sin of abortion. Their lives are just as valuable. However, there is a deafening silence from Catholics.

Jesus Christ, Our Lord, calls each one of you to be different to the rest of the world. It is the same call He gave to the apostles and to the disciples. He called us aside, not to be the same as everyone else but to be signs of His loving forgiveness, of His mercy. The early Church did that unto death but today so many of us just blend in with everyone else. We accept what everyone else accepts, we do not want to be different, seen as crazy, as religious nuts. So often we agree with what everyone else agrees with, because, "Well, they all agree with it, it must be right, mustn't it? Yes, let us abort the babies. Yes, let us vote for pro-abortion politicians. Yes, let us kill these people where the terrorists may or may not have come from!"

I am sure when the events in the Middle East change and America seems not to be winning or the cost is too high, many of those who support the war now will change their tune and become opponents of the war. What this shows is that these people are easily led by public opinion instead of being led by their faith. This is not what Christ calls us to. He calls us to a different life, a Christian life, to be Christlike. Until you do that, you are Christian in name only, you are playing at being Christian. Our Christian faith, our Catholic faith, the true faith, must be every moment of our lives. Not just in church. Not just in the sacraments, which are the greatest gifts of all. But every breath you take must be for Christ, every heartbeat you have must be one of love and forgiveness, reaching out to your brothers and sisters in love. It is when you live that way, you truly are imitating Christ.

VII

It is always a pleasure to be with holy people because your holiness radiates and touches me.

The saints and Our Blessed Mother encouraged me to think more in prayer about the merciful love of God and to see how that mercy was working in my life as God forgave me and embraced me in His love. That I, too, as a Christian, as an imitator of Christ, must open my heart to everyone in love and forgiveness, no matter how they treat me. That even if someone were to kill me, with my dying breath, I should pray for their forgiveness and I should forgive and love them as this is what Jesus did, and as an imitator of Christ, this is what I should do.

In the beginning, I found this extremely hard because there were so many people I was angry with. I would get frustrated very easily, impatient, often seeing the bad in others and not the good. Still I struggle with these things, but God has shown me that in myself, I will never overcome these but in Him, it is possible to. So every time now I have bad feelings about others, impatience, anger, frustration, one of the first things I do is look to Jesus on the cross and offer Him all the bad feelings that I have. I ask Him by the grace of His Holy Spirit to lift these from me so that I can show love and forgiveness. I have found the more I do this, the easier it seems to become.

Today I look at so many of you religious people, priests and nuns, and I see the good and holy lives that you lead. I also see the pressure you must be under at all times because truly, you are the front line troops of God, and being so, you would get the most attacks. It may happen if you live together in community, that you get impatient with each other, a little bit angry at times. You should understand that these thoughts coming to mind are often prompted by satan because he wants to distract you from your holy life. As when he draws a religious into thoughts of self and into thoughts of frustration and anger, resentment, then he places a barrier between them and God. The barrier that we are trapped in stops God's grace filling us completely and it stops us offering our life back to God completely because now we are trapped in these little frustrations. That is all they ever are, little things but sometimes we can make these little things seem so big. I have come to realise that the largest problem in the world, compared to the love of God in my life, is so small.

Saint Teresa of Avila very early on taught me an important lesson. She taught me that evil will always be there trying to distract people who want to live in the love of God. That we should try and recognise when these attacks are happening and once we do, then to ignore them and look past them and look to God. For if you keep thinking about these attacks, the distractions that keep happening, then you are not thinking about God you are thinking of them and that is what evil wants.

So saint Teresa said to me, "Always look beyond those, anytime there is any difficulty, any attack, first look to God and focus on Him." Once you do that and you call out from your heart, your very soul to God that you love Him and need His help, by the power and the grace of His Holy Spirit, He reaches deep into your soul and lifts you beyond yourself, beyond any distraction, deep into the holiness of His love. So that holiness now can fill your very spirit, your very being and you can reflect that holiness to others. As His holiness fills you, it brings you to what you are meant to be, an image of His merciful, forgiving and eternal love. When you allow this to happen within you, your soul burns so brightly that it disperses all the darkness around you and then the attacks that happen seem like nothing. It is then through the peace of that light of God within you, His grace reaches out through you to touch others. As they are touched by God's grace within you, they start to live more and more in His grace and now like Mary, your soul begins to magnify the grace and the love of Our Lord.

For the religious, you can do this in a very powerful way. Because as you are devoting your whole life, every second to God, in every second this light can shine brightly within you and in every second, the more you focus on God, this light can shine brighter and brighter so that one day, when people look at you, all they see in you is the love of God. For priests, of course, this is a wonderful thing to have within your parish because now as you pray and your soul brightens in the light of God, the whole parish comes to life in this love. It is by this light that you will lead others from the darkness and into the glorious love of God.

Those sisters living in community, know by your prayers, by your devotions, the light of Christ shines so brightly within your community and that it pours throughout the world to touch many souls. As I travel the world, I meet many people who say, they never knew God – like I did not – and then all of a sudden, one day, God touched them and they fell in love with Him and they do not know how or why it happened. Well, it is because of the grace that is poured out through people like you living for God. That grace, that light is shining brightly from this community and explodes like a shower of love around the world to touch many souls and bring them to salvation in Christ, Our Lord. So do not ever think that nothing is happening. Do not ever think that you are here in community and you cannot seem to do anything, or think that there is so much more that you should be doing or not much is happening by your efforts. If you devote your life totally to God in your community, then He uses you to pour out that grace and you become powerhouses of His love and in that way, you become part of the salvation that Christ offers mankind.

While this may be a struggle at times and there will be crosses to carry Our Blessed Mother, Mary, said to me once that when you can thank God for the crosses that you carry, that you show you are worthy to carry them. So whenever God gives me crosses, I thank Him, and as I thank Him, He fills me with the joy, the strength to carry anything and God will do the same for you when you thank Him for your crosses.

The motto of the World Youth Day (WYD) in Sydney was to receive the power of the Holy Spirit and to be witnesses to Christ to the ends of the world. How did you experience WYD in Sydney?

I took part in the days in the diocese in Perth where I spoke to a group of young people there. The effect of WYD on Australia was incredible. On one of the secular TV stations, every day for the whole week they had WYD and programmes about the pope, the Church and various saints. So for Australian Catholics it was very uplifting.

How do you see today's youth? Are they on a good path or do they also need conversion?

Well, the youth today are very confused. This is the fruit of the 60s and 70s when people embraced what they called free love. Of course, it was not free, it had a high price to be paid and the price is the change in society, which is bearing bad fruit today. This is because so many of the young people have not been taught any morals, they have been brought up to accept so many wrong things and they have not been set good examples. So if the youth are confused today, we cannot put all the blame on them. The blame is on the generation of the 60s and 70s who allowed the seed of confusion and of sin to be planted in so many lives.

I meet many young people as I travel and they are nearly all looking for something. They know there is something missing in their lives and many of them realise the things of the world really are not so important and they are searching for other things. Our duty as Catholics is to go out and help them find God and not let them be led into the New Age, which really is "old" age, or into eastern mysticism. We have to try and put right what has been put wrong in the 60s and 70s by giving clear, loving, gentle advice and being good examples to the young.

I have the impression that it is not about morals in the first place but about our relationship to God. How can this relationship be established?

Well, if you do not have morals, then God gets pushed aside. When you find true morals you find God because they come from Him. That is why I say Catholics have to be good examples because by living their Catholic faith and leading others to that faith, they bring morals back into society. So, as examples of Catholicism, we become true examples of love and true examples of how to live, to live the way of Jesus, which is the perfect way of love, which has no immorality in it.

Do you think WYD has helped the youth all over the world to start anew, to progress in faith?

Yes, I do. The Catholic youth that were there were a great example for everyone else and I have heard many young people talk about it, even those who are not Christian or Catholic and I have not heard a bad word about it. Everyone was saying how good WYD was, even the police in Australia were so surprised. They said that normally, if they have a few thousand young people together, that there would be many problems with drugs, with violence, with crime. But with half a million people there for WYD, they did not have one problem and they were so surprised at how well-behaved Catholics were. That in itself was a wonderful example to everyone else.

Our topic is: The Holy Spirit in my life. Can you tell us how the Holy Spirit works in your life?

From the beginning, the Holy Spirit has been helping me as He helps everyone. When heaven first came to me, I was told that God calls us to a partnership with Him. He never expects us to do anything by ourselves, that He longs to help us with everything and so I should ask the Holy Spirit to help me in everything. So I do that and whenever I am falling down, wherever I am failing, the Holy Spirit is always there to help as He is for everyone.

When I first began to pray, Saint Teresa of Avila told me that I should ask the Holy Spirit to help me pray because if I tried to pray by myself, I would be easily distracted, drawn into thoughts of self and the world. She said that I should ask the Holy Spirit to help me keep my focus on God in prayer and that would help me past these distractions and I found it was so true.

When I asked the Holy Spirit to help me pray, even though there were many distractions in prayer, by the grace of God I could look beyond those and keep my focus on the Father and the Son and the Holy Spirit. With my focus on God in prayer and not on self, by the grace of the Holy Spirit, my heart and soul opened to God and so God reached into my heart and soul and allowed me to experience what prayer really is – a joyful gift from God. As the Holy Spirit touched me within in prayer, He filled me with joy and any time I pray and ask the Holy Spirit to help me, that joy fills me. However, when I pray and forget to ask the Holy Spirit, that joy seems not to be there.

Now that joy is there for everyone. Prayer should not be a burden or a chore, it should be joyful, filled with peace and you can find that joy and that peace if you ask the Holy Spirit to help you pray. Now every day I ask the Holy Spirit to help me in every thing I do and because of that, every day is full of joy.

Is the Holy Spirit always "visible" or able to be sensed, or do we have to live in faith and trust?

For me, I see Him at times as a dove, as flames or I can feel Him at times as a wind, a gentle wind touching my face. But for most people, it is not like that. For most people, it is living by faith, trusting in the Holy Spirit. They may not experience what I experience, but at times people do feel the touch of the Holy Spirit. When I meet the people who have, it is so obvious, you can see the result in their eyes, in their faces because when you have had a touch of the love of the Holy Spirit, it changes you forever. Then you never want to lose the Holy Spirit again. As I look at these people, I think it is they who are the truly holy people because they may have never seen the Holy Spirit and they live in faith and in trust without seeing. Yet, for me, I had to see. I had no faith, I had no trust. It took the Holy Spirit shaking me up before I took any notice but these other people, so many of them, they just love God, they have that faith, that trust without seeing and they are the holy people.

Why is it that some can experience the Holy Spirit so strongly as you do while others can't? Don't the youth of today also need that experience?

Well, it is all down to free will. God gives us all free will. Throughout the life of everyone, God is reaching out to touch us with His Holy Spirit and to fill us with His divine graces and gifts. It is up to the person to say yes to it. God will not force Himself upon anyone.

When God came to me, He would always – and He still does – give me the choice to say yes or no to Him. He does not force me to do anything. I pray every day that I can say yes to God. He told me that if I want to keep my relationship to God, I have to live my Catholic faith in the sacraments, in prayer, in Holy Scripture and with a complete obedience to the Catholic Church.

Now sadly many people who are touched by God in their lives, sometimes do not realise what is happening and so they soon push it aside because they have never heard Catholics or Christians talk about the Holy Spirit or about what the Holy Spirit does. Which I actually think is a disgrace because all Catholics should be out opening their hearts and explaining Jesus and the power of His Holy Spirit to everyone.

It seems many Catholics who get touched by the Holy Spirit, by their own free will, say no to the Holy Spirit. When the Holy Spirit touches you He asks you to go out and share His touch with everyone, to share the love of God with everyone. Many Catholics say no to this, as they are afraid that they would be thought of as crazy, afraid of what the world would say about them or do to them. So they say no to the Holy Spirit and still they think they are living the faith. That is the problem in the world today that many Catholics are saying no to God and because they are going to church or praying, they think they are saying yes. But to say yes to God is not to just live your faith in the church, it is to live it in your life, every day, every moment and to share it with every person. Sometimes when the Holy Spirit touches Catholics they decide not to be obedient and so they deny the Holy Spirit.

So the reasons why many people are not filled with the Holy Spirit are varied. But these are some of the main ones; they say no to God when He reaches out and touches them, Catholics do not go out telling people of the Holy Spirit and what a person should do when the Holy Spirit comes to them. Or they refuse to be obedient to the Catholic Church.

You told how the Holy Spirit helps you in spiritual life, does He also help you in your relationship to others?

Of course He does. As the Holy Spirit touches you, He takes the scales away from your eyes so that when you look upon another person, you only have love for them for you see that each person is a creation of God's love. Loving God, you love His creation and you see each person is an image of God, created in the image of God, and so how could you not love His image? You see that God loves each one as He loves you and if God loves them, you have to love them.

So you just look upon each person and see the beauty of God's creative love. Now no longer do you have bad thoughts about others and no longer do you have jealousy. All you have is love for others. Seeing the sinner, even those committing the worst sins, you no longer condemn them or judge them but you look and see a person who is weak and you see how evil has manipulated the weakness to draw the person into sin and away from God. You have a burning desire within to pray for that person, to be converted. You long for that person to find the true way in life, the way of Jesus. You realise as well that you have your own weaknesses and it is only by the grace of God that you are not that person, that sinner. So when the Holy Spirit touches you, you just love everyone.

Is eternal love the real love that begins right here on earth?

Yes, this life is part of eternity. While it is just a moment in eternity, just a blink of an eye, it is an important moment where we can grow in the love of God, grow in His grace so that His grace can reach out through us and touch others and draw them to His eternal love. Once you realise what this life is, your fear of death goes away because you realise that everyone dies, it is part of living. It becomes clear that when you die, living for Jesus, that death is not a curse but death is the doorway to heaven. That through death in Christ, Our Lord, we come to live that glorious, eternal life in heaven. So this life is part of eternal life, but it is just a moment in eternity.

How do you see the role of the Church in this life?

The role of the Church is essential. The Catholic Church is the Body of Christ, it is the house of the Father, and it is filled with the Holy Spirit. If you want to come to God in eternity, you have to come to God in this world and God in His fullness in this world is in the Catholic Church. It is here where God resides in the Eucharist and so the Church is essential in leading us closer to God and in explaining to us how God wants us to live. The Holy Spirit speaks through the Church, explaining to us how to live God's way in everyday life so that we can come to Him in eternity.

As the Church leads us into itself and into the sacraments, we are filled with the grace, the strength and the love of God. In the Eucharist we are filled with God Himself who then resides in us every moment, helping us to live His way. The Church is the Body of Christ and we are all called to be one in His Body if we want to live as He asks. So it is impossible to live the way of Christ without living the way of the Catholic Church. All those other denominations that are not Catholic, while they may live some of the way of Christ, Our Lord, do not live the full way of Christ. A person can only live the full way of Christ, can only live the fullness in Him in His Holy, Catholic and Apostolic Church and nowhere else.

How do you see the future for mankind and for the world?

I think it is a wonderful future. So often we have forgotten everything is in God's hands and I see His hand at work now. As I travel the world, I meet so many young people who have been touched by God, so many who are looking for God, so many who realise that the way of the world is not the right way. The spring time Pope John Paul II spoke about has begun!

This is the beginning of it. The pendulum is swinging back to the way of goodness. It has been so far in the way of badness, but now God is starting to bring us back to Him and so I see the future of the world as wonderful. I see so much hope in the youth and I know that one glorious day in the future, Jesus will return and on that day, everything will be beautiful.

There is also lots of poverty in the world still. Shouldn't we try to limit that by God's help?

Well, naturally we should. If we are Christians, if we are Catholics, that is what we are meant to do. We are meant to help the poor and the needy. That is what Christ does and that is what He calls us to do. Yes, there are many, many suffering in the world today and they suffer because of the greed and selfishness of others, those who have so much.

In the Western world, we have plenty and we waste so much and what we waste would feed the Third World. If we only ate what we needed we could feed the Third World. If we did not buy new cars and new houses so often or spend so much on entertainment, we could feed the Third World.

In the USA, what they spend on their lawns is more than enough to feed all the poor in the world. There is enough for everyone but due to the selfishness and the greed of some, many suffer. There are such sinful things for example in the European Union where they have food mountains, where at times they destroy food, where they sometimes say to farmers, you cannot grow food on your fields because it does not suit policy – and yet people starve?

This is the blind pride and selfishness of the West. However, the problem is not only the West. In the Third World, there are many corrupt people who have been blinded by evil and drawn into selfishness and greed. Catholics as a whole should be praying for this corruption to be removed from the Western world and from the Third World so that all we have could be shared equally and so that all could have good and full lives in Christ, Our Lord.

God gives us enough but sadly our selfishness and greed takes much away from those in need. We cause the problem and we are so blind we cannot see it.

Let's come back to how the visible and the invisible world are inter-twined, maybe you can speak about the saints?

The saints are wonderful reflections of God's love. As you look at the saints, you see how each one of us can be holy in God. All the saints had weaknesses except Our Blessed Mother, Mary. All the saints had difficulties but they all overcame them in God by living totally for Him. So for mankind they are a wonderful example that no matter who you are, no matter what weaknesses you have, no matter what sins you have committed, if you embrace God completely, you can be a saint and you can find heaven.

A last word about the Holy Spirit, as we come to end of this interview …

The Holy Spirit is reaching out to every person, reaching out in love, saying, "I have everything you need. I want you to have a happy life, a good life, I want you to have everything in My love. Yes, you will have struggles in life, yes you may have crosses to carry, but if you let Me, I will be there to help you. I will give you the strength you need. I will give you the gifts and the graces you need. I will give you the love you need because I love you."

The Holy Spirit is love and all He wants to give each person is pure love so that in Him, they can find purity of life, happiness in life, in Him they can find eternal life in Christ, Our Lord.

Several TV stations in the United States as well as in Europe, Australia and in other countries aired interviews with Alan. The following compilation goes more in depth into Alan's story while it also contains helpful insights for anyone who is on their way towards holiness in this life.

You tell us in your talks that you were a swindler, a liar, an alcoholic, an all round bad guy.

I was not very good. Let's say if there was a scale of one to ten of being good, I was about two. I was deep in the gutter, I was very violent and addicted to many things and I hurt many people in my life.

How old were you then?

It actually began very early on. My father was a violent alcoholic who gambled the money away and we did not have much as children. He used to beat me (usually when I had done something wrong) and he was also violent towards other people. As I grew up, I saw that other people in London where I lived at that time which was a quite violent area, that other people respected him because of his aggression. So in my mind, it sunk into me that if I was aggressive, if I was violent, people would respect me. So it was very easy for me to come along and imitate him and be as he was.

This began very early. We did not have much money because what my father did not drink he gambled away. So when I was young

I decided that if I wanted money and things of the world, I had to get them myself and the only way I knew to get them was to steal. So I stole from everywhere and anyone, any opportunity I got I would steal. I even stole from the church until I got caught by the police. This was when I was about ten years old. Two big policemen jumped out of the confessional box and arrested me as I took the coins out of the candle box.

I had to go before a magistrate. That stopped me from stealing from church but I continued stealing from other places. I went before magistrates several times but for some reason, I never seemed to be sent to prison even though many of my friends were. I just got these warnings and fines and things and I could not understand why I kept getting let off while my friends were going to prison. Yet, I did not get sent there. I seemed to be left free to create chaos wherever I went.

I was part of a motorcycle group in London of which some were addicted to drugs, alcohol, violence and many other things. My life just revolved around all of that. My best friend went to prison because of murder and one of my closest friends was murdered. That was not uncommon. Around me many people were injured, were hurt in the violence we committed. So it was a difficult time full of sin and empty of God.

You were Catholic, weren't you?

Yes, I was a baptised Catholic. My mother is a true saint, she is an Irish Catholic from county Kerry. God must have given her a special strength to put up with our father and with us. She tried to live her faith always and bring us the faith.

My mother is like Saint Augustine's mother. She was praying for me for about 20, 30 years and finally her prayers were answered and she is very happy now.

How many siblings did you have?

I have four brothers.

It seems you had a really rough childhood in comparison to a lot of other people.

Well, now I look back and I think it actually was not so bad. I go to Africa and I see the children in Africa, and compared to my life style, they are far worse off than I was. At that time, I felt a lot of pity for myself and I wanted to prove myself and some of the ways to prove myself was by having lots of money so I would steal that. If you have money, people would think you are great. Being violent people were afraid of me they seemed to show some sort of respect.

When did you actually start drinking?

I started drinking when I was twelve. I just seemed to be drawn into it. It seemed exciting, it seems to make you feel good and you would not worry about things, but then the next day, you always felt miserable. It seemed to draw me into doing more bad things. A lot of the bad things I did was when I was under the influence of alcohol.

What kind of bad things are you talking about?

A lot of stealing and an extreme amount of violence. Later I joined a motorcycle gang and my best friend and protector, he murdered a man. Another good friend of mine stabbed a policeman, another friend of mine drugged an old lady so as to rob her.

You said in your talks that you also almost killed two or three people. Was it then?

What happened was, at about the age of 18, I decided to start learning martial arts because my protector had gone to prison and now I was coming up against some bigger people and it was getting a bit difficult. So I decided I would learn some martial arts and I studied them (Aikido, Aiki - Jutsu, Judo, Ju-Jutsu and Kendo) for 23 years and achieved a fourth degree black belt in one martial art. I was captain of the Australian team in the World Championships in 1992. I learnt these martial arts to improve my violence. During several fights with bigger people, I really lost my temper and it came to the stage that with just one more technique or punch and I would have killed them. They were beaten and bloodied and helpless before me. But something

inside me said, do not do it, and I just stopped. Sometimes right at the last moment. At times I would feel very sorry for these people because they would be in a very bad state.

You met your wife. Did you then change your life?

It was just about that time that my wife came over from Australia. When I first met my wife, I was 18 years and she was only 16. Her brother Stuart had just died and she was emotionally very fragile but I only showed her my good side if I had any. She did not know how bad I was but later on she found out as time went on.

Things were quite difficult in England at that time, it was in 1974 when I got married. I did not have a good job and it was very hard to survive. I was very angry with everything around me. My wife suggested, "Why don't you come to Australia and see what it is like there?" So I migrated to Australia in 1976.

It got worse there as Australians, many of them were very heavy drinkers and I fitted in really well. I drank more and more. The more I drank, the more violent I got and the more people I hurt. I would go to night clubs and fight with people – the bouncers we call them, the people who throw you out if you cause problems. I would fight those and many other people.

By then, you were a salesman for a pharmaceutical company?

God must have had His hand in my life already, because I was a man with no education. I mean, I left school at age fourteen. I got thrown out and expelled for stealing from a Jesuit School. I had no education. All I had was sort of my wits and I could talk to people okay I suppose.

Then this wonderful job came along. I was in Australia, a new country, and no one knew what I was like. I went to apply for this wonderful job and I thought I would never get it. I went along and there was a man who had gone to the same school as me in London, but he did not know me and so he gave me the job and it went on from there. I decided then I should study. I spent a lot of time studying medicine and the job went very well. I kept the good job that I had and I had a high salary in Australia, so I went from being very poor in England to having lots and lots of money. But I spent a lot of that money on alcohol and other things and so my bad life continued.

The job went well, but your personal life was still in shambles. How would your wife respond to all this? Did she have any faith at all?

At that time, my wife was a Protestant and she had more spirituality than I did. She is Catholic now and I thank God for that. She became Catholic after the change in my life. Before she used to say to me, "Why not go to church?" So I would go at Christmas or maybe at Easter and that would be it.

Wives who have husbands who are violent and alcoholic and do other things, I think God gives them the grace to carry these crosses. I have seen it in my mother, I saw it in my wife and I have seen it in other women that I have met. I think what happens is, often unknowingly, the wives open themselves up and receive the grace to carry their cross in a wonderful way. When we got married, she always said, "Marriage is for life." Even though I was very bad, I also thought marriage was for life. I do not know why but I just knew that. She seemed to be the stronger one emotionally and carried the crosses I put upon her very well. The worse I got, the more loving she got, the nicer she got.

Really? She didn't scream back at you?

She did sometimes. I remember once she lost her temper and I locked myself in the toilet.

You, the martial arts expert. That is good …

I look at the women, at the wives that I meet who have husbands that are alcoholic or violent or gamblers and treat them very badly and I pray for those women a lot and I can see a wonderful grace in those to carry on through their troubles. They are carrying their cross with Jesus and God pours grace through them in abundance, He really does.

The sad thing is that many people, when they see someone who is a violent alcoholic and who is married to this woman, they see the woman as the same. This is not the case at all. Often, because one person is bad, they think the other one is bad as well. That is certainly not the case. Many of those women are true saints because they put up with so much. They put up with it for the sake of their marriage, for the sake of their children, for the sake of love and they just persevere through difficulty.

How many years were you this really tough husband?

For 18 years but now it is wonderful.

Did God talk to your wife and prepare her?

In the beginning she found it hard to accept – one moment I was a drunkard and a fighter and doing so many bad things and the next minute I was a fraction better – my wife found the change really hard. She left me for three days once as she said, "You love God more than me." It is true, but she did not understand in what way at that time.

Jesus said to me, "Do not ignore your wife, do not ignore your family. Love them. Spend your time with Me but spend time with your family as well. My love helps families to grow, it does not destroy them. Do not be talking about Me all the time to your wife. Give her some time because she has not gone through what you have gone through." I used to lock myself in the room for hours, writing and I would talk about God all the time. The Lord advised, "Just step back a bit. Show your wife your love and show your children your love. Do not deny your love of Me but do not overpower them with it. Give them time. Pray for them."

So I did that and for a long time, we hardly spoke about God at home. I would be going to Mass every day and receiving the sacraments, going to prayer meetings and doing my writings. Whereas with my wife, I was rarely speaking about God and I just tried to show by the way that I lived God's love. The Lord Jesus explained, "Express My love by the way that you live, in everything you do. Use your love as an example. Show her how you are changing in My love and love her as much as you can. Love her more and more each day."

So I started to do that and I found a complete change. Before, when I used to pump God down her throat all the time, she turned away from me. But as soon as I stepped back and just showed love, things changed and then she became a Catholic on Corpus Christi. Sometime ago, the Lord filled her with the Holy Spirit. She was in ecstasy for hours and she came to love God and to understand everything.

How long did it take for you to turn your life around?

It was God who turned my life around, I just went along with it. I did not turn it myself. Saint Teresa began appearing to me in early 1993. At that time, I was addicted to alcohol. The moment I started praying the rosary, that addiction was taken from me straight away. One day I was addicted, the next day I had no desire for drink at all. All I wanted to do was pray. From the moment I started praying the rosary, my life started to change for the better. The love of God lifted me beyond the traps of the world and set me free in Him. All I had to do to find this wonderful gift was to do what I was created to do – to love God.

How long did it take for my conversion? I say that my conversion is every day. Today is the day of my conversion. I was told that I must look at my life in that way and every one should. Sometimes we say we were converted five or ten years ago and then it is easy to get into this routine and feel secure and feel you are living the right way. But when you look to every day as being your conversion day and you look to yourself and see how you are living each day, all of a sudden you realise how far from God you truly are. So when was I converted? Today!

Every day must be a day of conversion. It is when you think you have had your conversion experience, and you do not need to work at being converted again, it is then through your pride that the evil one can draw you away from God. Every day we need to be looking to how we are living, and see, are we living for Christ or are we living for self. If we are living for self, we must turn to Christ, Our Lord, every day and beg the Lord to heal us and convert us.

We all need to do that for every one of us is weak, human and fragile and in every day, some way, we are drawn into the world. It is in those moments that we need to turn to God and say, "Lord, help me, bring my focus on You and not on self."

Every day Catholics need to change because truly, many are not living the way of Christ. They are living the way of self and the way of the world and delude themselves into thinking they are living Christ's way.

So it was saint Teresa of Avila who played a major role in your conversion ...

At first an angel had been speaking to me, encouraging me to change my life. The angel left me after a while because I would not listen. Then I heard another voice, a strict, stern female voice, and she said she was Saint Teresa of Avila. She said, "Pull yourself together! This is the chance God is giving you for salvation and you should take it because if you do not, there is a good chance you are going to hell. The life you are leading is one that is going to lead you to hell."

I replied, "Well, I have just been told by the angel that God loves everyone and if God does love everyone and His love does not change, how can He condemn anyone to hell?"

Saint Teresa explained that we condemn ourselves to hell by the way we live. That throughout their lives, God is always reaching out to every person offering them salvation, offering them guidance to walk the right path to heaven. God in His divine love wants no one to go to hell, He wants everyone to live in His eternal love in heaven and that in His love He gives everyone the free choice to accept that or not. I was told I was making the wrong choice. Today many people in their pride, in their self, turn away from God's helping hand and they keep stumbling along on the path that leads to hell.

That was what I was doing and now heaven told me I needed to change my life because if I did not, by my free choice, by my free will, I was walking the path leading to hell. But that God was still reaching out and calling me back to the true path, the path of Jesus. I did not believe in hell and she explained it to me in great detail, it really shook me up.

During the time when the angel at first came to you, you also had to suffer attacks from the evil one. How did you experience that? Was he like a physical being?

Oh yes, he was. I could not touch him but he could touch me. That continues. I think what happens is, when God tries to come into your life and when God does come into your life in a certain way to bring you closer to Him, evil tries to stop that happening. I think that is what was happening at that time. It was frightening me, it was really frightening me and in my fear – and I had not known much fear, I was not really frightened of many things before but now I was afraid – I would turn more and more to the booze. So I carried on drinking and doing all the bad things.

You were really a target in a spiritual battle between good and evil at that moment, between the good trying to get your soul and evil trying to catch your soul. There was a war going on there …

It is a war that is going on in everyone's life to a lesser or greater degree. I have come to understand that every second of our life, there are evil angels around us trying to attack us and destroy us in more or less subtle ways. Sometimes not so subtle, I have met several people who have had physical attacks as well.

But it is a constant thing – we have God's angels there guarding us and protecting us and there is this constant battle as they fight to keep evil away. That is why it is so important that we should thank God for the angels He sends to guard us and to look after us. Sadly, often people forget that.

I remember once I was in my bedroom at home kneeling down praying the rosary and all of a sudden, satan was there and he started to attack me physically. Then Saint Michael the archangel was there and he was protecting me. Then there were lots of evil angels, hundreds of them, I do not know how they would all fit in the room but they were all there. They were all attacking me, kicking me and beating me. Then, all of a sudden, there were lots of God's angels there. There was Saint Gabriel and Saint Raphael and hundreds and hundreds of God's angels, more and more of God's angels and all the evil angels just got pushed away. I was just surrounded by all God's angels joining in the rosary. That was wonderful.

At which point did you actually go to a priest?

I had no thoughts about going to church but Saint Teresa, Saint Andrew, Saint Matthew, Saint Stephen and Saint Thomas who were with me at that time, they encouraged me to go to church. There was a little church around the corner called Our Lady of Victory's, and a beautiful old Irish priest who is dead now, Father Sean Sorahan, one of the most wonderful priests you would ever meet.

I went and saw him. I thought he would think I was crazy. I sat down and told him what was happening. He was uncertain until the Lord told me something about him that happened in his life when he was young and I told him about that. Then, all of a sudden, he believed. He sent me to a theologian to speak to. Then, later heaven encouraged me to go and see Archbishop Barry Hickey, which I did and I explained everything to him.

He appointed a spiritual director, Father Gerald Dickinson, who is dead now. The archbishop is very wise. He appointed someone who did not believe in me. When I saw Father Dickinson, the first thing he said was, "I do not believe in you. I do not believe in all this." However, within a couple of months, he became my strongest supporter and he was up to the day he died. He was a wonderful spiritual director. He was very strict, very clever and very spiritual.

There is God's wisdom again. He got someone who did not believe and He turned him around and made him completely believe.

So you began going to church and your spiritual life was completely turned around?

Yes, it was. Now I started to go first to Our Lady of Victory's and as I was looking to the statues, they began to come alive and I began to see many saints, all the apostles. They were all giving me the same message, but in different ways. For me, that was an interesting thing because then I began to understand that in each of the saints, God shows us a different way to come closer to Him, a different aspect of His love. But the message is always the same and the message they were giving me is, "Love God first and foremost, above all others, above all else, even above yourself. Place God first in all things. Love fellow man, and you must live the sacramental, prayerful, scriptural life with that total obedience to the Catholic Church." Over and over, this has been the message, and it has never changed. It has been in different ways, but that is always the basic message.

Till today, you have locutions, visions. Many people can't believe this, they think it is fantasy.

The first time I experienced this it was an interior locution, but then I began to see and hear audibly. I wondered at times if it was just me seeing things but as time went on, people that I would be with, if I was having a vision, sometimes they would see it as well. I also thought, well, even if I am crazy, every vision and locution I am getting is all about goodness and love and is bringing me to a happy life and every time the Lord, Our Lady or a saint appear or are speaking to me, I am so happy. So I thought, if I am crazy, I do not care.

When you say locution, is it a voice in your heart, something that you do not visually see?

The locutions I can hear audibly as I hear you or it can be in my head. I can have one or two people speaking to me and at the same time I can have my own thoughts.

How often do you get locutions or visions?

Every day and it is from when I wake up in the morning till I sleep at night, interspersed throughout the day, and even in my dreams.

The Lord tells me that this will continue as long as I continue to live my Catholic faith, receiving the sacraments, reading Holy Scripture, praying and being completely obedient to the Catholic Church. The Lord said, it is my choice every day. If I choose to live this way, then it will continue but I have the free choice not to live this way and if I choose not to then it will stop. So I ask you to pray that I make the right choice every day.

You also had encounters with Our Blessed Mother?

When Our Blessed Mother started speaking and appearing to me, she told me she is my mother, she is everyone's mother. I call her mum. She is absolutely wonderful. She is there in all sorts of times, especially when I am in trouble. She says she is there to bring every person closer to God the Father and the Son and the Holy Spirit. That is the reward God gives to her because she was so obedient to His will in her life that now, God allows Our Blessed Mother, Mary, to bring us closer to Him.

Every time she speaks to me, it is never about herself but always about the Father and the Son and the Holy Spirit, it is always about God. She is always directing my vision, my focus to God. She said that is what she wants to do for every person.

You said she came in your times of need. What need are you talking about?

When I have my dry and dark moments, she is there encouraging me. When I sometimes feel a little bit of self pity ...

With all the graces you are given, what would cause the dry moments?

A dry moment is if I am not having visions. I may still be having locutions, but I might not have a vision for two or three weeks and I might feel sorry for myself. I am having locutions every day and all day, it never stops but sometimes I may not have a vision for some time and I would think, oh, what is going on? I would feel so bad and far away from God. This is because even though the locutions are wonderful the visions are more powerful and I feel closer to God when they happen. Maybe this is a weakness of my pride where I want to see God more and do not appreciate the locutions enough. During these times also there are many attacks from evil.

Why and since when do you travel the world giving talks and praying for people?

I have done it from 1994. The Lord told me from the beginning that He wanted me to do His work. He said it would never be easy – believe me, it is not. He asked me if I would give my life for Him. As I had fallen in love with Jesus, I could not say no. He said, "Giving your life for Me means going out, sharing My love with everyone. Devote your life to this so that others can find the happiness and the peace that you do in My love." I could not and did not want to say no to Jesus because I love Him so much. I just want to please Him. Also inside me, feeling this deep love, this deep joy, I just wanted everyone else to feel that as well and so I willingly go out for Him. People ask me, "When will you stop?" I stop when the Church asks me to or the day I die.

In order to go out for Jesus, you quit your job and gave up financial security. What did your wife say to that?

When I said to her that Jesus asked me to do His work and that I should leave the high paying job I had, she said yes straight away. She actually was a fine example for me. There was no question, no doubt because a few months before that, she had been filled by the Holy Spirit during one of my talks. She was not a Catholic but she became Catholic and she fell deeply in love with Jesus as well. So she is happy to do whatever Jesus wants, no matter what it costs.

Was it difficult to start going out? How did that go?

It was difficult. I had never spoken to big groups of people before and it was the last thing I truly wanted to do. When the Lord asked me to speak, even though I was extremely nervous, and I still am at every talk, I got up and let Jesus give me the words. Seeing so many people touched by His love in His words just made this desire inside me, that desire to share His love, it just made that stronger.

You said you quit your job. What do you live on with your family?

I trust in God, I never ask for money from anyone, I just go out and speak and pray for healing and I leave it up to God. He has never let me down. Sadly sometimes I let Him down. He never lets me down and He gives me all I need.

You wrote a book called "Through the Eyes of Jesus". It contains conversations between Jesus and the apostles and things that happened as they walked the Holy Land, is it some sort of extension of the Bible. Why would Jesus give this to you?

First of all, let me say that it does not compare with Holy Scripture, that is the sacred Word of God. Jesus gave me this to show some of the things people maybe wanted to know or needed to know. What it does in the apostles and the way they related to Jesus, it shows all our weaknesses and yet how Jesus helped the apostles through their weaknesses to become such strong and powerful men.

It also shows in Judas that Jesus continued to offer His love to Judas. He never stopped loving Judas, always He loved him deeply. How Judas in his weakness, in his selfishness, in his pride kept turning away from God. Jesus is showing again in Judas' life that it does not matter how bad we have been, He still constantly loves us. All we need to do is turn back to Him. So in some of the apostles you can see that they turn back through their weaknesses to Jesus and they become very strong in Him and this can be the same for us. Or with those like Judas, those who turn away, then of course you get weaker and filled with more pride and self.

There is a story when Jesus and the apostles were tired after a long day and some mothers brought their children and the apostles wanted to turn them away. What is the theme of this story for us?

For me, one of the things that came out of this was: Often you see children in church running around, screaming, crying and carrying on. You may also hear people complaining about them and saying, "Why can't the mothers carry them out, they should not be here." But God does not say that. God is happy that they are there, whether they are screaming or shouting, He is just happy they are there and He wants the mothers to bring their children to Him. What this shows is that some people in the church have the same pride where they do not want those children to be there because it is disturbing their time or relationship with God. Yet, God is calling those children to Him and in those other people's relationship with God, they should see this as a way of sacrificing. They should say, "Yes it is disturbing a little bit that these children are here, but I offer it to You, Lord, as a sacrifice because I know You want to fill these children with Your love and bring them closer to You."

So, there are a lot of comparisons in there. Also in the apostles trying to keep the others away, trying to keep the mothers with children away. This also sometimes compares to people within the Church and in different denominations, people who think that God is just for them, for this select few people, because they are holy and not like others. They think God is just for this group of people because they pray and go to church. They forget God is for everyone.

How did you write that book? Did God say, "Alan, you and I are going to write a book together?"

Well, I write all day and every day. God gives me a lot. There are about 8000 pages of writing at the moment. When He gave me the book Through the Eyes of Jesus, He started showing me, it was like a movie screen before me. It was like watching a movie, but I was in the movie. Then, at other times, I was in or amongst the apostles. I was actually at times inside Jesus and looking out through His eyes and experiencing a few of His emotions. There was so much happening, many ways to experience what was being revealed.

I remember one particular man in the book who had abused his daughter, she got pregnant and the baby died and then the daughter died. Jesus confronted that man in a loving way and the man now saw the wrong that he had done. He placed a knife on his heart and was just about to kill himself. At that moment, I was inside that man and I could feel that knife touching his chest. I could feel his anguish and I knew he would push that knife into his heart and kill himself.

In that moment, Jesus looked into his eyes, looked into his soul, and at that moment, the man knew the loving forgiveness of God and

185

he did not kill himself and he changed his whole life. He now helped young women in need and young children in need and that was all through the loving mercy of God. To experience that and to experience that feeling within, I could again feel that loving forgiveness of Jesus which I felt earlier myself. It was wonderful to see that 2000 years ago, people were experiencing the same thing.

People say today, oh, the world is much worse than it was before. But, you know, it is the same sin, it is not new sin, it is all the same. It is the same problems, the same concerns. Maybe there is a bit more of it because it is more obvious and with the technologies, we can do a few more wrong things and spread them quicker. But the basic sins are the same.

God seems to grace people like you in special ways, more than ordinary people

One thing I have to say is, with a visionary or a locutionist or a stigmatist or someone who is gifted with healing or any of the other gifts, all this does not make them a special person. Often I see many people, they look up and say, "Oh, that person is a stigmatist, there is a visionary, I have to listen to them," and they follow blindly what this person is saying. Yet you should not do that!

In God's eyes, we are all equal. He loves you as He loves me. Yes, He is expressing certain gifts in my life, but it does not mean that He loves you less or that I am holier than you – I am certainly not holy. I am trying to be, but I do not think I will ever be. Sadly, many people look to those having visions or locutions or with stigmata and follow everything they say without question. You should not do that. You should first check everything with the teachings of the Catholic Church. If anything goes against that, you ignore it and you ignore that person. If it is in line with Church teaching, then you can listen to it but it must be Holy Scripture and Church teaching first.

There are healings, heaven seems to confirm your ministry. How did the healings start?

It actually started in Father Richard's parish who is my spiritual director now. However, this was before he was my spiritual director.

It was about 1995 when the Lord started to ask me to pray with people for healing. So I started to do that and nothing happened. I thought maybe I got this wrong and I said to the Lord, "I am praying for healing and nothing is happening." He said, "Just keep on doing it." So I continued and nothing happened. Again the Lord said, "Persevere." So for about six or nine months, I was doing it, praying over lots of people, yet nothing happened.

Then one night I was giving a talk in Father Richard's parish and as I was praying over people, for the first time, many of them fell down. Actually I think about 90% of them fell down, that is a lot. It was almost as if a bomb had hit the place and knocked everyone down. That night, people started to claim healings. People were healed of cancer, a cripple walked, a deaf person heard.

The Lord said to me what He was calling for was my perseverance and trust in Him. He told me that He would heal through me and nothing happened. But because He asked me to, I persevered and by His grace, I trusted in Him and when the time was right, He began to heal people. Again it shows when you persevere and just trust in God, when the time is right, He will do what is necessary.

It is the same for everyone, if we persevere and trust, God will give us the gifts we need. Since then the healings have continued until today. The Lord tells me as long as I continue to trust in Him, to live a sacramental life, to pray, to read Holy Scripture and be completely obedient to the Catholic Church, then all the gifts will continue. It is my free choice to do that or not.

So every day, my prayer is that I can continue to persevere in loving God and I ask everyone who hears or reads this to pray for me that I can. I am weak and human and at times it is easy to fall down and I hope I will not and I trust God will give me the strength to persevere in the sacraments.

Some Catholics or Christians have problems with people falling down in the church. What do you say to them?

Can you imagine how I felt when I was praying over people and they were falling down? I had never experienced that before. It was a shock but as I looked at them, they seemed to be at peace and they looked happy. Later the Lord told me, that sometimes what He does, He sort of puts the person's mind out of the way, to take away the barriers the person has so that He can work within them for healing. Often when that happens, that is when they fall down.

When I pray with people, I only touch them very lightly with a finger on the forehead so it certainly is not me pushing them down. Sometimes my prayer is only for a second and sometimes they fall down before I am even near them. But it is not the falling down that is important. What is important is that people let God do what He wants to do. When He wants to put you down, let Him, if He does not, that is fine. The important thing is, just let God have complete control of your will. Sometimes when I pray with people nearly everyone falls down, other times almost no one falls down. However, that is not important to me, the important thing is that people have come for Mass, have listened to the talk, that they have a good confession, that they are there for the exposition of the Blessed Sacrament and also they get my very insignificant prayer. So I do not care if they all fall down or no one falls down. The important thing is they are there for the sacraments.

Did God tell you that He was preparing you to be an ambassador for Him for other people? Because you are doing this full time now, to share God's love and win souls back for God. Did He tell you that was what He had in mind for your life?

He did. The first time Jesus came to me and asked me, would I do anything for Him, overwhelmed with His love, how could I refuse Him? I answered, "What ever you ask, Lord, I will do it. Even if it costs my life, I give my life to You, it is Yours." I pray I can keep that promise and I pray that till the day I die, every moment can be Jesus'. I hope everyone will pray for me that it will be that way and I will pray that it will be like that in your life and everyone else's life.

Did God show you your future?

He showed me what my future can be if I hold on to His love. It can be a glorious one as it can be for everyone who holds on to His love. It can be one with peace, with joy, with happiness, contentment. I experience that every moment in my life, no matter where I am, even in the most dangerous situations I feel at peace, I feel happy, I feel secure. He says to me that if I continue to live for Him and to work for Him, that, of course, the final reward is heaven as it is for everyone who loves God. I said to Him, "I will be happy if I can just scrape into the lowest part of purgatory. I will be very happy with that because then I know that I will be going to heaven." So, if I could get there, I will be happy.

Do you yell at your wife anymore? Do you still sin?

We used to argue just about every day. But now we argue maybe once in a couple of months or something like that, very rarely. These are small arguments usually, but before it used to be really big ones. That is what God does, He changes us and takes the bad things away. Unfortunately I won't stop sinning until the day I die. I have this terrible pride where at times I feel better than other people. I do not want to feel that way but it seems to be within me – yet I know I am no better than anyone else. It makes me cry at times that I can think that way – how could I think that I am better than anyone? In God's eyes, we are all the same and if God sees everyone equal, then I must see everyone equal. We are all God's children, but for some reason, I get this terrible feeling inside me at times and it really breaks my heart to have that because I do not want to have it. I pray that God would take that away but He does not seem to and I cannot seem to get rid of it. That is a cross.

You said it was the message of a loving God. Is there a special message for German speaking Europe or for Europe? What does Jesus say?

Whichever country I go to, they all ask me, is there a special message for this country? Yes, it is the same message for every country: Love God, love each other and live your Catholic faith. If you do that, your country will change and the world will change, it will change for the better.

Often people are looking for more in the messages that God has given throughout time. They are looking for more mysterious ways and they forget the most important commandments: Love God and love each other. That is our faith and if people in every country would start to live those two commandments, then life would be better. So that is the message of God, love Him, love each other, and this is especially for you and your country.

X   A BRIEF INTERVIEW WITH ALAN'S SPIRITUAL DIRECTOR

Father Richard Rutkauskas, is Alan's present spiritual director. Together, with Archbishop Barry James Hickey, Father Richard works out the guidelines for Alan's ministry. He does not only give Alan advice in spiritual matters, but also checks all Alan's writings before publishing and, if time allows, he also accompanies Alan on his trips overseas (Africa, Europe, America ...). The following is a short interview Father Richard gave in Europe during one of Alan's visits.

Father Richard, you are a priest, working in a big parish in West Australia. Archbishop Hickey made you Alan's spiritual director. When did you start to do this work and what does it comprise?

It was after Fr. Dickinson died I took over and it is very easy to be the spiritual director of Alan because Alan is a very nice person to work with. He is never very demanding and I just give whatever support I can to him.

What sort of special tasks do you have as spiritual director?

Like I said before, it is mainly to support Alan in his spiritual life. When he writes down things, I make sure that what he has written is in following with the Church's teaching.

If someone has visions, the Church has to check. What does the Church say about Alan?

The official Church does not make any judgement. Usually you will see that if something like this happens, while the person is still supposedly having visions or locutions, the official Church will never make a judgement.

Are there experiences that touched you personally very deeply?

For me, the most important experience is to see people going to the sacrament of penance because quite often, at the various places where Alan speaks, the Holy Spirit touches hearts and quite often people are coming to the sacrament of penance after many years.

Father Richard, have you ever had a supernatural experience yourself, a vision or the like?

Over the years, maybe a couple of times some small things happened like I saw a blue light. I had my eyes closed as Alan prayed over me and this bright blue light appeared. His wife who was with us had exactly the same experience at the same time but for me, such things are not important. Personally I received a special grace last year (when I was with Alan), possibly when I was in Austria. I have been a priest now for twenty years and from the beginning, I have been a nervous preacher. I always used notes when I preached but I received the grace last year and now I do not need notes and I am more confident in preaching.

Many people are sceptical when lay people pray over others and do this ministry of prayer. Are there guidelines from the Church for this?

I think so long as anyone comes under the authority from the Church, especially their own archbishop or bishop, as it happens in our diocese our archbishop gives full permission for Alan to speak and pray over people for healing. Archbishop Hickey has appointed me to be Alan's spiritual director so that I can have a close eye on him.

(The Vatican gave guidelines for Healing Masses which are not in the Mass Book, but there is no restrictions as for non-liturgical healing prayers – and that is what Alan does. Anyone can go and pray for healing in the church with non-liturgical healing prayers and pray in this way for others and with others if the priest-in-charge allows. In some places, though, the bishop might want to be asked first and give his explicit permission. However, local priests would know how it is handled in their diocese and parish.)

When travelling, people from all ranks and of different cultural backgrounds come and ask questions. A selection of those follow here, assorted according to topics.

—   *Family and experiencing God*

What is your testimony about life in marriage and family?

I am married and I have two adult children. My wife, when this began, she was a Protestant. But after she saw the change in my life and what God was doing for me, she became a Catholic, which is wonderful. But again, in the beginning, when all this was happening, first I was overwhelming her with information. The Lord said, "Do not do that, step back. Live your marriage, your sacramental marriage in Me, and it is through that you will bring her to Me. Show love at all times."

He said, the marriage, it is a Trinitarian celebration of love with God at the head of the marriage, and then my wife and myself. In everything in the marriage, I should put God first and think of God first. In doing so, that would bring His grace into everything in the marriage. So I started to do that. Now before that, we used to argue just about every day. But the Lord said to me, "Realise when you are having bad thoughts, when you are arguing, disagreeing, getting angry, realise how much you are hurting Me in your marriage. Because your marriage should be a gift of love that you offer to Me but when you are arguing, when you are behaving badly, what sort of gift are you bringing to Me?"

So every time I started to feel bad and wanted to argue, I would think of God and how I would be offending Him by doing this. Suddenly, I did not want to argue any more. My wife could not believe it. So the arguments got less and less and we started talking about love more in our marriage and our marriage became very strong.

Again it was by showing that love in my life, the love of God, and bringing that into our marriage, that God reached out and touched my wife and brought her to fullness of life in Him. So in my marriage, God is first. My wife never used to understand that, she used to ask, "Do you love me more than anything?" I used to say, "I love God and then I love you", and that confused her. But now when I say that to her, she says to me, she loves God and then she loves me.

So, putting God first in all things brings change, brings peace, brings fullness into people's hearts. This is what Jesus showed us in His life. He put the Father in the first place in all things and we must do the same.

Do you still see your friends you had before?

Two of them I do but most of them still carry on as I did before so by choice I do not see them. They think, "He has gone crazy, he has gone religious."

How is it to hear God speak to you?

It feels wonderful, it is the greatest feeling. Apart from receiving Jesus in the Eucharist, the greatest feeling is to be filled with the Word of God and be filled with the Holy Spirit. It is the most exciting thing. It sets your heart on fire and nothing, nothing in this world compares to it. It goes beyond anything you could experience with drugs or alcohol. It goes beyond anything in this world. So even at times when I may look tired or I may look down, inside me there is an excitement, a fire burning because God is filling me with His Holy Word. I pray that everyone could experience that, because if they did, everyone would be living for God in every moment.

When Jesus comes to you, how do you react, do you kneel down?

Someone said to me, "Shouldn't you be on your knees all the time!" It is not like that. When Jesus is with me, He is my friend. I have the respect for Him as He is God and I know He is everything but He says to me, "I am your friend. Talk to Me as your friend and know I am your best friend." I talk to Him as I talk to you. He is my friend and He loves me so much. Of course, I do not lose any of the respect for Him being God. Often He overwhelms me with ecstasy. Sometimes I feel I could die when I have that ecstasy and He tells me, "This is not even the smallest touch of heaven." It is the same with Our Blessed Mother. She is just there as a loving mother and she makes me feel so happy.

The Lord said, "This is how your relationship with God should be. Knowing that Jesus is your friend, your brother, and He wants to be there to help you and make you part of His family. The Father is your father and He wants you to speak to Him and talk to Him as a father because He loves you as His children. The Holy Spirit is there to fill you with love and you should just speak to Him in a loving way and accept His love."

I was told that when I share God's love to just speak normal. You do not have to put airs and graces on. Just be normal, just be yourself because that is the way God has made you, to be yourself. That is what God told me from the beginning, He said, "The only thing I want to change in your life is the sinning. I want you to stop the sinning and start to live a holy life. I want you to remain the person that you are because that is how I have made you. So do not try to make yourself something you are not. Just be yourself." That is a problem many of us have, we try to make ourselves something that we are not.

You mentioned that after your conversion, your son got so sick that he was in danger to die. If he had died, how would you have felt about that?

If he had died, I would have been sad but I would not have turned from God, believe me.

What about the martial arts? Should people do that?

I was captain of the Australian team in the World Championships in 1992 in a martial art called Aikido in which I have a fourth degree

195

black belt. I have studied it for 23 years. It was a big part of my life but when God came to me, I came to see that this is nothing at all. Martial arts are actually a deception to lead us from God. So often, it is told that martial arts are going to teach the children discipline and that it is going to help them defend themselves. Actually all it is doing is to teach you to hurt other people. It is just one of the disguises again, you know, "It is for their best, it is for their good." But it is not at all, it is teaching you to hurt people.

So often I have seen people who have learned martial arts and then they are using it to hurt people. Children should not play martial arts, no one should play martial arts. There should not be martial arts. I do not do it now and I encourage no one to send their children there because they also get taught these eastern influences like Shinto or Buddhism. They are being taught that it is okay to hurt people if you are doing it to defend yourself, it is okay to do all these terrible things. Martial arts are wrong. They take you from God and they teach you to hurt people. So no one should encourage their children to go there and if your children do go, encourage them to stop doing it and come back to the Church instead of going to martial arts. Learn the discipline of Christ.

— *Spirituality, faith and prayer life*

What can I do to lead people who are dear to me back to God?

The first thing is, if you try to force people to love God, it never works. If you try to bring them to God by fear, it never works. Once they get over the fear, they go back to what they were doing. The way to bring people to God is by love. So you must show them love and forgiveness at all times. Never condemning them, never judging them, because we never have the right to do that. By the example of your life, by showing the love of Christ in your life to them, this is how you lead them back.

Also, by continuously offering the Eucharist for them. I have done this with people in my own family, and it has taken some time, but it has had miraculous results because the Eucharist, of course, is the most powerful prayer of all. So I continuously offer the Eucharist for people in need. Then I do not keep worrying about it. I know that by offering this most powerful prayer, that now these people are in God's hands. It is then by me showing the example of Jesus' love in my life to these people, I know I am by the grace of God, planting a seed deep inside their soul that God, one day, in His eucharistic love will bring to fruition. Now I may never see it, I might die before I see these people change. But I know and I completely trust in the Eucharistic power of God, that by offering the Eucharist, these people will be changed and even if this is in the last second of their life, I will be happy.

I would like to share one example with you. My father died last year. All my life I had known him as a violent, alcoholic gambler. He had some bad experiences in the war that disturbed his brain so he lived an extremely bad life. Even up to six or seven months before he died, even though he was dying with cancer, he was still leading an extremely bad life. He did not believe in God. He said, "How could there be a God who would let war happen and people get killed?" He thought anyone who believed in God was crazy. I wondered how I could get him to change before he died. He seemed so stubborn, so hard. But I kept praying and offering the Eucharist.

Then, one day suddenly at the end of one of the sentences when he was talking to me, he said, "God bless you." Then he started to talk about God. Then – he has five sons – he bought each one of us a crucifix with our names on them. He had always made a promise he would never have the Last Rites, that he would never go to Communion or Confession. But he did all of those. The last two months of his life he was extremely happy. The nurses at the hospital said, they had never seen someone die like him, he was so happy.

He also said he would never have any flowers at his funeral. Now, he had never heard of divine mercy. Even though I prayed the Divine Mercy Chaplet for him, I had never mentioned it to him. It was three days before he died, he said, "I will have one red rose and one white rose on my coffin." When I saw that on his coffin, I knew that God was being merciful to him and I know, if my father can be converted like that, anyone can.

How can we get the youth come to Sunday mass and receive the sacrament of marriage?

It is very difficult because today the world has seduced the young. What we should do is keep offering their lives to God. Every time we receive Jesus in the Eucharist, we say, "Here, Lord, they are Yours, I give them to you. I leave them in Your care." Then all you do is live your faith, being an example for them, no matter how hard it gets, no matter how much it hurts you inside when they refuse to listen to you, when they make fun of you and think you are crazy. Just see they are behaving like this because they have been blinded by the world.

You keep looking to heaven, keep offering them to Jesus in the Eucharist, and then, do not worry, trust in Him. Know that some time in their life, God will touch them, God will give them a great opportunity to change. All you need to do is keep praying that they will accept that opportunity. So the answer is, offer them in the Eucharist to Jesus, be an example by living your faith and stop worrying and trying to force them to change. You cannot force people to love God, you can only lead them to the love of God.

Someone is involved in New Age and I cannot help.

Never argue with anger, never hate, never resent. That is not from God, it is not from Jesus at all when you do that. God is love, understanding, caring and forgiveness. God only has the right to judge and condemn. Jesus has said to me so many times, "When you see people like this, love them, understand them, care for them, offer them your love, explain God's love. Explain where they are going wrong. Do not force Me upon them. Just explain and show them by the example of your life what God's love truly is because so many people misunderstand it. When they are involved in those new age things, it is so important that you pray for them and understand that your prayers will be answered."

So often, we are praying and praying and nothing is happening. Then we may think to give up as God is not listening to our prayers. Well, God is listening, and He works in His ways and in His time. It is up to you to persevere and not to give up. It is when you give up you are losing trust and hope in God and this is what evil wants. So when you get frustrated and you start to feel angry as no one is changing and they are going down the wrong path, that is satan having a victory in your life. You have got to keep praying, you have got to offer the sacraments for these people. You have to trust that God will bring them back in His way and in His time. It is so important we do that, yet it is so hard, isn't it?

How do you know the will of God if everything seems to be going wrong?

First of all, the will of God is that you love in all situations, even when it is difficult, when it is hard, when you are struggling. So you have got to focus first of all on loving God and loving each other. To know the will of God is very easy really, but we make it very hard. You just have to look to the Catholic Church and to the teachings of the Catholic Church and follow those and lead a sacramental life. So, if you live in love and live in obedience to the Church, then you will have peace in your heart. When that peace is disturbed, you know you are going the wrong way. The peace that God puts there through Catholicism is the peace that tells you everything is fine. So when you feel that peace, you know you are doing God's will.

Do we have guardian angels?

Yes, we do, and we should never forget our angels. They are gifts from God, there to protect us, watch over us, to guide us, to help us in our lives. So often we forget them. They are from God, filled with His love, and they surround us with His love and protect us against so many things that we do not see nor understand. We all have angels and every day, we should say a prayer for them because they love to hear that.

What is it like seeing an angel?

When you see the angels of God, you feel the presence of His love through them. They are always shining so brightly and there is a warmth that comes from them. They are often there when I am in troubles, protecting me.

When evil is around, always God's angels are there protecting us. They always remind me that God sends them and that they are there by God's love and God's grace. Every time they speak, everything is focused on God to magnify God's love.

How can we walk the good way?

We all have a choice. There is always the choice to do good and bad within us. It is there and we have the choice to go down the good path or to accept the bad path. God gives us the grace, if we ask Him, to walk down the good path but in humility, we have to turn and ask Him and recognise that we have these choices of good or bad.

So many people say to me, "You should not watch television." There is nothing wrong with television, believe me. If you watch the right thing, it is a wonderful instrument, but so often we watch the wrong thing. There is nothing wrong with television but with what is on, you have to be selective.

People say, "You should not go to movies." There are some great movies but I am very selective with what I watch. If you are selective with what you watch, then there is nothing wrong with it. You can choose the bad ones and that is your free choice. There is good and bad in everything. To condemn something because it is being used for bad is to condemn something that could also be used for good.

So in life the choice is ours to do good or not, to walk the right way or not.

Have you also seen Saint Peter?

All the saints that spoke and appeared to me were telling me who they were but one saint would never tell me who he was and it was going on for about a year. I would see this short man with a bald head and quite stocky, with a moustache and beard, and he just appeared and never said anything. I was asking all the others, "Who is he?" They never told me. I was getting really frustrated because I wanted to know who he was and then one day Saint Peter spoke to me and gave me this message:

"A long time ago I was there but you did not recognise me. You looked, you saw, but you did not know. Know me now and join with me in singing the praises of the Lord God, Jesus, Christ, the true Messiah, the true Lord and the true God.

"Jesus, Who, with the Father and the Holy Spirit, is the true God. Our Lord, Our Saviour, Our Redeemer, Our God. Jesus, Who wept from His heart for mankind, wept tears of blood, tears of love. Jesus, Who loved completely His family on earth, loved all, no matter who or what they were. Jesus, Who offers salvation to all, not just a few. Jesus, my Lord, my God, my Master and my dearest friend whose forgiveness knows no end. Jesus Who says to all, 'Become My new apostles and follow Me.'"

When you do pray the rosary, do you feel the light of God around you?

When I pray the rosary, I feel the love of God deep inside me, I feel warmth all around me, I feel joy, I feel happiness, I feel love and many wonderful things happen. When I pray the rosary or any prayers, I always ask the Holy Spirit first to lead me and guide me in prayer, because in myself I cannot pray properly. It is only by the grace of God I can and so I ask the Holy Spirit for that grace every time I pray.

What if you fall asleep when praying the rosary?

I often fall asleep saying the rosary. This is okay, because you have the intention of saying the rosary. If you fall asleep in prayer, I mean, you are going to be in the arms of Mary.

Sometimes when I come into the church and I am sitting there quietly in adoration I fall asleep. I woke up once and I said, "Lord, look, I came here to be with You and I fell asleep!" He responded, "Well, if you cannot fall asleep in front of your best friend, who can you fall asleep in front of?"

How can you offer each second to God while at the same time walking around, talking, working ...

First of all, God wakes me up early every morning. Even if I have gone to bed about 2 or 3 o'clock, He will wake me up around four or five in the morning. I start my day by saying my 45 decades. Then, I find it very easy to continue praying throughout the day. The reason I find it so easy is that every morning, the first thing I do, I turn to the Holy Spirit and say, "Lord, I cannot do this myself. You will have to help me, You will have to show me." So every day He does. When I am speaking to people, often as I am speaking, I am thinking each word that I am speaking is a prayer of love to God. Any time I am working, every movement, every part of the work is a prayer to God. Every day I try and serve people as much as I can because I know then I am serving Jesus. If you ask God to help you and try your best, you will be surprised what you can do.

I enjoy life, I watch movies, I watch television, but you can do that and still offer those moments to God. I am very careful in what I watch and what I do, but I live a normal life. When I go back home, my wife and myself go out to restaurants, we go to the movies, we go bowling and do all sorts of things. God does not mind. He is quite happy that I am enjoying myself. He wants everyone to enjoy life in goodness and in love.

— *Questions about healing*

What about the gift of healing? How should we go about our health, also as religious? What is the relationship between body, mind and soul?

First of all, the Lord said that any baptised Christian, that any baptised Catholic is filled with gifts and graces and that any of us who pray for healing in the name of Jesus, the Holy Spirit will work through to heal others. So it is not only me that has the gift of healing but it is all of us. I am always surprised because so many people come to me for healing prayers and by the grace of God, there are many, many healings.

But I am so disappointed that people do not go to priests because whatever graces and gifts God gives through lay people, He gives stronger through the religious, through the priests. It is only the priests, it is only their hands that by the grace of God can change the bread and wine into the Body and Blood of Jesus. So that shows the enormous power in the priest's hands by the grace of God. So I think everyone should be going to the priests for prayers of healing, before coming to people like me.

Now with our body, our mind, our spirit, our soul, it is all one and we have to treat each part of it properly. That means, for my body, I have to eat properly and exercise properly. I remember once Our

Blessed Mother said to me when I was overweight, she said, "Eat less and exercise more."

Also, for our mind, of course, we have to exercise our mind as well with good reading, good thoughts, I do that by reading Holy Scripture but you can do it by also reading many wonderful books that will stimulate your mind to think more and more about God. To exercise and use your mind correctly, whether it is in mathematics, science, English or whatever, the first thing you must do is, put God at the centre. Asking God to help you understand what you are reading, what you are studying so that you won't get led down the wrong path but follow the path that God has given us in knowledge.

Spiritually, you have to exercise to grow spiritually. There are many of those spiritual exercises that the saints have told us about. Of course, they centre on prayer, Holy Scripture and on the sacraments. One that I find very difficult at times is trying to humble yourself before others. As you start to put others before yourself, as you start to lift others up to God before yourself, your spirit is strengthened in the grace of God. Strengthened to be able to lift more and more people up to God by lowering yourself to serve them and help them, imitating Christ in what you do. So as you lower yourself below others, you can see yourself as being lowered below the cross, to lift others up as Jesus lifted up the cross and in that way, you can carry the cross of Jesus in your life.

Can one receive prayer in proxy, rest in Spirit in proxy?

When you stand in for other people, the prayer and the grace often flow through you to touch other people. It happens very frequently that people are standing in for others and then rest in the Spirit and then sometimes within a few days, within a few weeks and even within a few years they hear from the other person they were standing in for and they hear of a good change in their life. So it is quite possible that your resting in the spirit was for the person you stood in for.

Why is it that some people aren't healed immediately but only days, weeks or months later?

Sometimes people say to me they were not healed for some months after I prayed with them, and they wonder why this happens. I ask them, "What did you do different after I prayed with you?" Some say, "I went to Mass more," or, "I went to Confession more," or, "I prayed more," or, "I stopped doing the bad thing I was doing."

Well, that was it! God has always called us to a partnership with Him. He calls you to be part of your own healing, to have an action of faith. In Holy Scripture, to the man with the withered hand, Jesus said, "Stretch out your hand," and in an act of faith the man did it and he was healed. To another one He said, "Pick up your bed and walk," and in an act of faith the man did it and he was healed.

For some of you, your act of faith may be increasing the sacraments, increasing prayer and most definitely stopping any bad things you are doing. It may be then when you do that act of faith that God heals you.

— *Priests and the sacraments*

What if one receives communion while in the state of sin?

As I said in the beginning, you have to be totally obedient to the Catholic Church. If you are living in a state of grievous or mortal sin, you really should not come and receive the sacrament because you are offending God. So if you are in a state of grievous sin, the priest should say to you that you cannot receive the sacrament until you have had a good confession. This is the teaching of the Church and you must be obedient to that.

Does the Lord want us to have more perpetual adoration?

Yes, He does. Adoration is wonderful. Every parish that has perpetual adoration seems to grow and grow because the presence of the Lord is there. The people loving and adoring Him become filled with His love and they touch other people with His love. It is so important that we do it. But also, perpetual adoration does not end when you are just in a church with Our Lord exposed there. Perpetual adoration should be in every second of your life because you should be adoring God with every breath, with everything that you do. When you do this, that is perpetual adoration in your whole life.

We are a dying nation with low birth rate and it looks as if in fifty years, Islam would take over from us.

It is very interesting because often when people in the West talk about the decline in birth rates and the number of Muslims, we forget about the people in South America, in Africa, in Asia, the Christians, the Catholics there, where the majority of the Church is. Their birth rates are not low. It is we in the West that have the low birth rates. One thing God said to me very recently, He said, "It does not matter if the whole world is controlled by those who do not know or love God. Whether they be Muslims, communists or masons. It does not matter, Jesus has won.

If these people take charge of the world, it will only be for a short while. The fullness of God's victory will come to earth regardless of what people do. They cannot stop it. All we have to do is continue to believe in that victory and live in that victory so that many more souls can be saved. Jesus always tells me, "Do not worry about those things. It is God Who is all-powerful, not man." That if I live for God and in God, then by His power, many more will be saved.

He also tells me I should not even worry about satan. That if I live in the Eucharist, I have the power of God, the power of heaven within me and no anti-Christ, not even satan himself can overcome that power. It is only my weaknesses, my fears, my doubts, that can change that. I tell you truthfully, if satan was to come right now into this church and there was just one of us living in the Eucharist, he would flee in terror. He knows he is beaten, it is he who is afraid. We should remember we have nothing to fear, we are the victors, we have won. Even if the world is controlled by those who do not know God, do not worry about it, keep living your faith and trust in the victory because God will make everything right.

Has Our Blessed Mother ever talked to you about abortion?

Yes, she has. In the book Messages, there is a beautiful message from her about abortion. She says this is a terrible sin. We are killing the next generation, we are killing our own children. She asks, why are we doing this? We are no better than they were in South America in former times with all the sacrifices they had there of the children. We are doing exactly the same today. We are killing our future, our priests, our nuns, our presidents ... We are killing our future.

I saw Our Blessed Mother once with her arms open wide to the aborted babies around her. She was crying as she said "My babies".

We are usually accepting or doing abortions because people want better holidays, better cars, better lives, better healthcare for themselves. People think they cannot afford children, it is going to invade their lives, causing some problems. People who call themselves pro-life at times vote for pro-abortion candidates and see nothing wrong in that. It is impossible to be pro-life and to knowingly vote for a pro-abortion candidate. How foolish! This is supporting and becoming part of this great evil. Often thinking about how a particular politician will improve their lives through maybe tax rebates, better health care or improving the economy and the poor babies are forgotten. This is self, self, self.

I encourage you, pray that abortion stops because it is a terrible sin, a terrible cross that we have to carry.

— *The evil one, the end times and the future*

What was satan like when you saw him?

I won't give you too many details. I can see a big fear in your face. Do not be afraid! He comes in all ways but there is nothing to be frightened of. He uses the same things over and over, the same tricks, the same deceptions. He works in the way of building up our jealousy and he offers us things to build up our greed, our selfishness. He offers us wealth, fame. He uses the same things over and over. His ways have not changed, they are still the same as they were thousands of years ago. It is so obvious when you see it. What you have got to understand is, there is nothing to be frightened of. You do not need to be worried at all. Trust in God. Do not worry about him at all. It is when you start worrying about him, you let him into your life.

Why didn't you describe hell?

I have descriptions of hell that were given to me by the Lord and also Saint Teresa showed hell to me. My spiritual director asked me not to explain hell to people. There is something better than that, a description of heaven in my book: "The Way of Hope".

I also used to think that going to purgatory was terrible, but it is not. In purgatory, you atone for your sins. The great thing about purgatory is, if you are going there, you know that finally, you are going to be in heaven. It is wonderful. So if I could just scrape into purgatory, I would be really happy.

What about the end times?

Many people are full of fear about what is going to happen tomorrow, next year, the year after. If the anti-Christ is coming, if all these bad things are going to happen ... You do not need to worry about this. If you are living close to God, if you are leading a sacramental and prayerful life, why are you worried? Jesus has promised you when you are faithful to Him and His way, He will take you to heaven. So if you die tomorrow, it does not matter, does it? Because we are going to a much better place, it is much better than here! So why are we worried?

It is only our fear, our insecurity and our weakness that allows evil to take hold of the world. If we live our faith strongly in the Eucharist, then this world will change. But it begins with each one of you saying your fiat, your yes, just as Mary did. Saying yes to live as Jesus calls you to. Live with a total commitment of being obedient to His will even unto death. When you live that way, then you will change the world by the grace of God. So do not fear the end times. You could die tomorrow of a heart attack, that could be your end time. Just live today for God. Do not worry about tomorrow.

Yet, so many people are concerned. This is satan taking hold of you. You are thinking of self. You are going to die. Your family, your friends, you worry about them, about what is going to happen in your life, that you are going to have no food, etc.

Do not worry about it! Jesus said to the apostles, "It is how you live today, do not worry about tomorrow," when they were asking the same question. But satan confuses many people and builds these fears up. Some people are beginning to live in caves and store food up. If you store food up, as a Christian, as a Catholic, if a disaster does happen, you cannot keep it for yourself! You must share it! If you do not share it, you are sinning. If you do not share it, people will know you have it and they will go and kill you and take it. So what's the point?

Also, God with the Jews in the desert, He gave them manna from heaven, He gave them water from the stone. He will give us whatever we will need. We do not need to doubt that.

Today, so many people are worried about the end times, worried about self. Yet there are the people in the Third World, the poor and the starving not having medicine to cure their simple diseases, and they are dying. They haven't got work, they cannot get food and they are dying! Today, we worry about ourselves, about us getting comfort in our cars, going on holidays, our food, and worry, "Are we going to die next year because of the end times?" We forget these poor people who today are living the end times. For them, it is the end times.

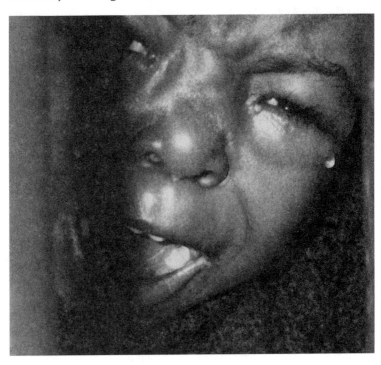

As Catholics, we should be forgetting ourselves and we shoı reaching out to those poor people, helping these people. Offerıng them our love, money, food, medicine, offering them whatever they need to overcome these difficulties so that they can live the good life, the life we have. How dare we think about ourselves? How dare we worry about next year, the year after, the end times when so many people today, in the Third World, are living the end times?

As Catholics, as Christians, we should be ashamed of ourselves for we allow this to happen and we worry about ourselves. Today, for the Third World, this is the end times. Stop worrying about tomorrow, worry about your brothers and sisters and reach out in Catholicism, in love, in God's love. Reach out and help them now.

— *The Church*

What should we do when there are errors in the Church?

The Church is full of sinners and by the grace of God, hopefully we all will be saints. God came to save sinners and He gives His Church to save sinners. Because it is full of sinners, yes, there may be mistakes, because we are human, we are weak. It is natural that we are going to fall down at times. If there are mistakes in the Church, we are not called to be angry. What we are called to do is understand that this Church is filled with the Holy Spirit and we should bow in humble obedience to the Holy Spirit. We should be praying and praying and offering the sacraments that by the power of the Holy Spirit any wrongs be put right.

The Holy Spirit, in His time and in His way, will put things right. What He calls for is us to trust in His divine power. Sadly today, many people see what they believe to be a wrong in the Church, they get angry, get frustrated and leave the Church. But because there may be wrongs that people might be doing in the Church, this does not stop this being the Body of Christ. Jesus gave us this Church with the full knowledge of our weakness. He hopes that unlike those in John 6, that people will not turn their back and walk away because they do not understand the mystery of this Church and because they are looking with human eyes and human weaknesses.

In the morals and teachings of the Church that were given by Jesus and the apostles there is no error. There might be a misunderstanding from us because we look with human eyes rather than asking the Holy Spirit to see with spiritual eyes. In the infallible teachings of the Popes there is no wrong.

Just because the world says it is okay to take things like contraception, or maybe okay to kill people, or to be homosexual, it does not make it right. Sadly today, many Catholics just want to blend in with the world and accept what everyone else accepts. They see the Church as a democracy that should suit them but it is not a democracy. If it were a democracy, it would be a people's church and protesting against God's will. They want the church to bend to their will instead of them submitting to God's will. This is God's Church, and it is not a democracy. God is in charge. In love of God people would want to be obedient to His will, to His teachings. In love of self and pride in the world, people want to turn away from God. This Church is God's, be Catholic and be part of God's Catholic Church.

In regard to frequent communion with Christ in the Holy Mass the Catholic Encyclopaedia says:

Without specifying how often the faithful should communicate, Christ simply bids us eat His Flesh and drink His Blood, and warns us, that if we do not do so, we shall not have life in us (John 6, etc.). The fact, however, that His Body and Blood were to be received under the appearances of bread and wine, the ordinary daily food and drink of His hearers, would point, to the frequent and even daily reception of the Sacrament. The manna, too, with which He compared "the bread which He would give", was daily partaken of by the Israelites. Moreover, though the petition "give us this day our daily bread" does not primarily refer to the Eucharist, nevertheless it could not fail to lead men to believe that their souls, as well as their bodies, stood in need of daily nourishment.

In the early Church at Jerusalem the faithful received every day (Acts 2:46). Later on, however, we read that St. Paul remained at Troas for seven days, and it was only "on the first day of the week" that the faithful "assembled to break bread" (Acts 20:6–11; cf. 1 Corinthians 16:2). According to the "Didache" the breaking of bread took place on "the Lord's day" (kata kyriaken, c. xiv). Pliny says that the Christians assembled "on a fixed day" (Ep. x); and St. Justin, "on the day called Sunday".

As time went on daily Mass did became the norm, but it is only recently in the Church's history (Pope Pius X) that the faithful have been urged to receive communion each time they attend Mass, not just once a year as was the custom.

The Catholic Catechism simply states:
1417 The Church warmly recommends that the faithful receive Holy Communion when they participate in the celebration of the Eucharist; she obliges them to do so at least once a year.

So, frequent Holy Communion is recommended but it is not necessary or available to all. Think of shift workers, those living in isolated areas, those looking after babies, sick, elderly. Also, If we cannot receive Communion physically, either because we cannot make it to Mass or because we need to go to Confession first, we can pray an Act of Spiritual Communion, in which we express our desire to be united with Christ and ask Him to come into our soul. A spiritual communion is not sacramental, but prayed devoutly, it can be a source of grace that can strengthen us until we can receive the Sacrament of Communion once again.

God bless,

Fr Richard Rutkauskas
5 Ingham Crt
Willetton WA 6155
Australia

Books available from:

USA   *Alan Ames Ministry*
                P.O. Box 200
                Kellogg
                Minnesotta 55945

                Phone: 507 767 3027
                www.alanames.org

AUSTRALIA   *Touch of Heaven*
                (Alan Ames Ministry)
                P.O. Box 85
                Wembley, 6014
                West Australia

                Phone: 61 89 275 6608
                Fax: 61 89 382 4392
                www.alanames.ws
                toheaven@iinet.net.au